ACID REFLUX DIET

Dr. Jessika Schwab

Legal & Disclaimer

The information contained in this book and its contents is not designed to replace or take the place of any form of medical or professional advice and is not meant to replace the need for independent medical, financial, legal, or other professional advice or services, as may be required. The content and information in this book have been provided for educational and entertainment purposes only.

The content and information contained in this book have been compiled from sources deemed reliable, and it is accurate to the best of the Author's knowledge, information, and belief. However, the Author cannot guarantee its accuracy and validity, and cannot be held liable for any errors or omissions. Further, changes are periodically made to this book as and when needed. Where appropriate and/or necessary, you must consult a professional (including, but not limited to, your doctor, attorney, financial advisor or such other professional advisor) before using any of the suggested remedies, techniques, or information in this book.

Upon using the contents and information contained in this book, you agree to hold harmless the Author from and against any damages, costs, and expenses, including any legal fees potentially resulting from the application of any of the information provided by this book. This disclaimer applies to any loss, damages, or injury caused by the use and application, whether directly or indirectly, of any advice or information presented, whether for breach of contract, tort, negligence, personal injury, criminal intent, or under any other cause of action.

You agree to accept all risks of using the information presented inside this book.

You agree that by continuing to read this book, where appropriate or necessary, you shall consult a professional (including, but not limited to, your doctor, attorney, or financial advisor, or such other advisor as needed) before using any of the suggested remedies, techniques, or information in this book.

Dedication

I thank my many friends and family members for their support and helpful suggestions: Kate, Rosy, Aly, Very, Simo, Rita, Marika, Gerry, Cynthia, Flo, Roby, and Alex.

I give thanks to God for the incredible energy, clarity, and support I received in bringing forth this book.

YOUR FREE GIFT

As a way of saying thanks for your purchase, we're offering
FREE PRINTABLE ACID REFLUX Grocery Shopping List (PDF file)
that's exclusive to readers of this book.

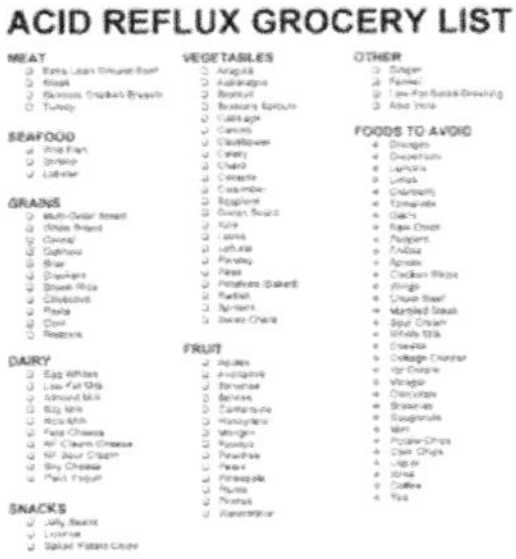
ACID REFLUX GROCERY LIST

MEAT

SEAFOOD

GRAINS

DAIRY

SNACKS

VEGETABLES

FRUIT

OTHER

FOODS TO AVOID

Free Download at

BONUS.JESSIKASCHWAB.COM

IMPORTANT

for corrections, suggestions and comments:
drjessikaschwab.books@gmail.com

Table of Contents

Introduction

Heartburn, acid reflux, or gastroesophageal reflux disease (GERD) is a pretty common medical condition, which causes stomach acid or bile to travel back up the esophagus and mouth. Usually, a small valve located at the end of the esophagus (where it connects to the stomach) prevents stomach acid and partially digested food from coming back up. However, some people have a weaker valve, or their valve does not close properly, allowing the contents of the stomach to enter the esophagus.

Because stomach acid is powerful, it can damage the delicate esophagus and mouth tissues, which are not designed to withstand an assault from such an acidic substance. Stomach acid that ends up in the mouth can also damage teeth. If you suffer from GERD, you may notice this reflux, which feels like an unpleasant burning sensation in your chest and throat.

Common remedies for GERD include antacids made from aluminum, calcium, magnesium or bicarbonates. These substances neutralize acid, preventing it from damaging exposed tissues. However, using antacids in excess can cause ion and mineral imbalances in the body, and most are very hard on the kidneys. A better solution is to control acid reflux with diet and lifestyle.

Chapter 1: The Acid Reflux Explained

Acid reflux is a medical condition that is associated with flowing up of the stomach acid, which is mostly composed of hydrochloric acid, into the food pipe, or esophagus. In some people, the acid reflux comes in between burping, which can be embarrassing, especially when eating in public.

The hydrochloric acid aids in proper food digestion and acts as a protector from bacteria. Our stomach is a complex organ composed of various parts. Its lining is designed to produce the acid that protects the digestive tract system against wear and tear, particularly from ulcers when there is not enough food to digest, as well as combatting H. pylori infection.

What Is H. pylori?

Helicobacter pylorus is a bacterium that may invade the body and dwell in the digestive tract. Its presence is not felt easily as it slowly harms the gastrointestinal tract by causing sores or ulcers. Some infection caused by H. pylori may cause ulcers, bleeding, and cancer and some may cause other symptoms. There are medications available to kill the bacteria and cure the ulcer. The bacteria come from poor sanitation and contaminated water.

Facts about Acid Reflux:

There are many things that every person should know about acid reflux that most people are unaware of. Here are the facts:

1. It has many names such as GERD or gastroesophageal reflux disease and heartburn. It is also called as acid indigestion or pyrosis.
2. The condition will be called GERD if acid reflux symptoms occur more than twice per week.

3. It is a common ailment among Westerners, particularly Americans.

4. The esophagus is protected by a gastroesophageal sphincter, which is composed of muscle, from possible harm brought about by the stomach contents. The muscle acts as a gate valve by blocking the stomach entrance.

5. Heartburn happens when there is abnormal activity in the gastroesophageal sphincter, where the acid from the stomach flows up into the esophagus or food pipe.

6. It is commonly felt after eating with symptoms such as burning pain around or below the chest area.

7. Smoking and obesity can trigger acid reflux.

8. It is treatable with over-the-counter medications and alternative medicine.

9. GERD can lead to complications, and the most feared is cancer.

10. Heartburn is not related to the heart, although the pain is below or around the chest area.

11. One can feel a bitter or sour taste within the mouth region and throat for a few minutes to hours.

12. Spitting more often by chewing gum helps a lot to swallow more acid and push the acid back to the stomach.

13. Sleeping with more than one pillow can relieve you of heartburn.

14. Wearing tight jeans and sleeping after eating can trigger heartburn.

15. It usually occurs after eating, sleeping after eating, and physical activity after eating.

Prevalence of Acid Reflux:

Based on the report made by the American College of Gastroenterology, acid reflux illness is common in the United States. Sixty million Americans can experience heartburn once a month.

Fifteen million Americans have symptoms of acid reflux almost every day. To sum it up, about 20 to 30% of the populations in Western countries are suffering from this condition.

About one in five Americans are prone to have heartburn, and one in six Americans have high risks of acid reflux or 40% of the adult population. Its prevalence has increased by about 50% from ten years ago in the Norwegian population based on a report issued by the medical journal *Gut* in the last quarter of 2011.

Who Is at Risk of Acid Reflux?

Acid reflux may occur at any age. Children can have it at a younger age, and some may experience heartburn as they grow older. You are at risk if you have any of the following:

- If you are obese
- If you are pregnant
- If you love to wear tight-fitting clothes, pants, and belts
- If you have a hiatal hernia
- If you are a passive or active smoker
- If you have a sedentary life
- If you have a low-fiber diet
- If you love spicy and irritating foods
- If you eat close to bedtime
- If you are fond of salty foods

Complications of Acid Reflux:

Acid reflux can lead to complications if it is uncontrolled and left untreated. Both esophagitis and Barrett's esophagus may lead to cancer in some patients. This is based on a 1999 study reported in the *New England Journal of Medicine.*

The study disclosed the connection between cancer and acid reflux. Patients are, therefore, advised to seek medical advice if their condition persists even after taking medications and applying home remedies.

In recent studies by the American Association for Cancer Research in 2013, it reported that there is a big possibility that untreated acid reflux may lead to cancers of the throat and the vocal cord. The same study said that antacids could help a lot in controlling acidity in the stomach.

When the symptoms of acid reflux persist for a week, it will develop into GERD or gastroesophageal reflux disease, resulting in more serious medical problems, such as:

1. Barrett's esophagus- This is a severe illness caused by chronic GERD. It can also occur in people who do not have GERD, but generally it can be a risk factor for Barrett's esophagus. Acid reflux can be the cause of Barrett's esophagus if it happens many times and lead to abnormalities in the cells found in the esophageal lining. The damaged cell will then be replaced with an unusual type of cells in the esophagus, putting the patient at risk of cancer. Not all cases of Barrett's esophagus will lead to cancer.

2. Esophagitis- This condition is accompanied by irritation and pain in the esophagus due to the backwash of the stomach acid. This is the result of pressure in the esophageal lining when the acid keeps on going back to the esophagus, causing ulceration, scarring, and bleeding. People who have esophagitis are at risk of getting cancer.

3. Esophageal bleeding- There are many causes of esophageal bleeding, among them is liver scarring. Chronic liver disease may result in bleeding that overflows to the esophageal lining, causing esophageal varices or enlargement of the veins. Aside from liver disease, stomach varices due to duodenal scarring and stomach acidity may also result in bleeding that needs prompt medical attention.

4. Ulcers- Acid reflux may develop into a painful sore in the gastrointestinal and esophageal linings. It happens when the lining becomes eroded because of constant pressure by the acid. Untreated stomach ulcers may become malignant. If you are having abdominal pain that does not stop, seek medical attention as soon as possible.

5. Esophageal cancer- When acid reflux becomes frequent, it will develop into GERD, causing irritation and bleeding in the esophagus as the stomach acid keeps on flowing back. Cancer growth starts from the cells in the esophageal lining.

6. Strictures- These are injuries caused by acid reflux due to the constant pressure of acid flowing into the esophagus. The acid will result in inflammation and scarring in the esophagus. Sufferers may have a hard time swallowing their food as they can feel the irritation when the food is stuck while traveling to the esophagus.

This chapter has been dedicated to the basics of acid reflux and symptoms to inform readers that this medical condition should be treated to avoid complications. In succeeding chapters, you will learn different tests and exams to diagnose acid reflux, homeopathy, alternative medicine, surgical options and postoperative care after surgery, and a dietary plan.

Symptoms of Acid Reflux

The commonly known sign is heartburn, which is often the only symptom people watch for when they notice the disease.

In a healthy individual, there is a ring of muscle that opens and closes in the lower part of the esophagus. It is closed most of the time and only opens when food is entering the stomach. This keeps all the acid in the stomach safely in the stomach where it belongs and away from the sensitive esophagus area.

When an individual develops gastroesophageal reflux disease, this ring doesn't work correctly, which allows the acid from the stomach to creep up into the esophagus. This results in all the burning and painful sensations you feel in your throat and chest—this is why many people refer to it as heartburn.

Normal heartburn only lasts for a short period and it doesn't reoccur. If your heartburn is prolonged and comes back often, you should seek medical attention as untreated acid reflux will often result in further complications.

Since acid reflux can cause different complications, it's essential to know what the other common symptoms are. This is one of the most misdiagnosed diseases. Many people live with it unknowingly for several years.

In addition to heartburn, other symptoms include:

•Stomach Bloating – bloating can be caused by several conditions, but it is often associated with acid reflux. If you often feel bloated, consult your medical professional as soon as possible.

•Frequent Burping – unexplained burping, painful burping, or burping that tastes bad are all signs of stomach acid being present in the esophagus.

•Dark stool – your bowel movements say a lot about your health. Dark stools often indicate that there is some problem going on with the digestive tract. If you are experiencing this at any time, consult your medical doctor as soon as possible.

•Dysphagia – difficulty swallowing will often indicate some poor medical conditions, and it's wise to consult a medical doctor as quickly as possible.

•Nausea

•Unexplained weight loss

•Unexplained or prolonged sore throat (or a sore throat that keeps coming back) – cold and flu season is one thing, but if you find that you have a sore throat—no matter how mild—that keeps coming back, go in and get it looked at by a doctor.

•Tasting stomach acid – this is one of the prime indications that there is stomach acid in the esophagus.

•Pain when you are lying down – lying down makes it even easier for your stomach acid to creep into your esophagus, especially when your sphincter isn't working.

Hiccups

Wheezing

Dry cough

Hoarseness of voice

Discomfort and burning pain right below the breastbone, and sometimes it reaches the throat area.

Whenever there is any change in your health or comfort, it's a good idea to get it looked at by a medical professional. Many conditions can contribute to these symptoms, but keep in mind that acid reflux could be the culprit.

If you are going to the doctor for any of these symptoms, bring up acid reflux if your physician does not.

Chapter 2: Causes of Acid Reflux

There is not one single cause of acid reflux, but it could be one or a combination of many factors causing the problem. It is a doctor's job to help the patient identify these possible causes to create a treatment plan. We will study several potential causes before jumping into any conclusions.

The most simple, widely accepted cause of acid reflux is the production of too much acid in the stomach. As food enters the stomach, it triggers the release of stomach acid into the mix to begin breaking down the food into smaller particles. The amount that is released is usually dependent on how much food and what type of food needs to be broken down. For example, low-fiber foods and simple sugars like refined flour products are quickly broken down into their smallest form and therefore do not require much stomach acid to digest. More complex particles, like animal proteins or high-fiber foods, will need a bit more acid to break them down. If this recognition system gets out of whack, food may trigger a release of stomach acid that is not appropriate for the food. When an overwhelming amount of acid quickly dissolves the food, it is released from the stomach into the small intestine. If the stomach is still producing acid on an empty stomach, it is likely to cause a problem. In the case where too much acid is produced, reflux symptoms are more likely to occur.

The pharmaceutical industry thrives on this concept, as there are several prescriptions and over-the-counter remedies that work by reducing stomach acid. The theory is that if there were less stomach acid altogether, there would be less that would enter the esophagus, therefore relieving symptoms and causing less damage.

Functional Issues Leading to GERD:

There are also many functional problems in the esophagus and stomach region that can lead to acid reflux. When food enters the mouth and slides down the esophagus toward the stomach, the lower esophageal sphincter (LES) opens to let the bolus (chewed mass of food) into the stomach, then it closes quickly behind the bolus, protecting the esophagus from any acid that tries to enter. The LES is finely tuned to open at the specific moment the bolus reaches it. If there is any confusion in this signaling, if there were nerve damage, for example, the LES may begin to open at inappropriate times, allowing stomach acid to enter the esophagus.

The lower esophageal sphincter can also become distorted or twisted, which does not allow it to close completely. This can either be a structural issue or stomach issues. When there is increased pressure in the stomach, it pushes up on the lower esophageal sphincter, opening it slightly. When the seal of the sphincter is compromised, any bit of acid that splashes up through it will cause burning and a painful sensation, usually called heartburn. Excess food in the stomach can cause pressure, usually by eating too fast. There may also be a functional issue with the stomach, which causes it to empty slower, allowing food to build up, causing the pressure.

A hiatal hernia is another possible cause of consistent reflux. A hiatal hernia occurs when you get a larger than normal opening in the diaphragm where the esophagus pokes through to meet the stomach. This extra space allows a portion of the stomach to protrude through, causing extra pressure on the lower esophageal sphincter. There is a high possibility of acid entering the esophagus.

A hiatal hernia can happen at birth or develop over time and can range in size, leading to different symptoms. Most hernias are harmless and go unnoticed unless a doctor suspects it is the cause of symptoms. Diet change can address most of the cases, but surgery can fix more severe cases.

Stress and Acid Reflux:

Stress seems to be a common culprit in many body ailments. It can cause headaches that turn to migraines, create fatigue, muscle aches, high blood pressure, and several other problems, including acid reflux and GERD. According to a 2011 study reported on healthline.com, there is a strong correlation between work-induced stress and the incidence of GERD. Participants reported a higher rate of GERD during times of stress. This study was completed in Norway with over 40,000 people. They also reported that low job satisfaction was a common thread.

Another study in 1993 shows that more anxious people reported a higher severity of symptoms than people who were generally relaxed. Interestingly, the study established no correlation between these increased feelings of discomfort and a tangible increase in stomach acid. This leads to the theory that stress must have some effect on receptors in the cells of tissue that makes them more sensitive to stimuli, creating the illusion of more symptoms. The doctors theorize that stress somehow turns up sensory receptors in the brain, causing more of a reaction than would normally be induced by a small amount of acid in the esophagus. It proves that symptoms can appear to be exaggerated during stressful times.

Note that the patients involved in this study already reported having symptoms of acid reflux and this was a study to determine the role of stress and increasing signs of GERD. It does not propose that stress causes acid reflux necessarily, just that symptoms can appear worse if stress is a factor.

Also, these studies are limited in that they have only reviewed the result of acute stress on acid reflux, like exposure to freezing temperatures or loud, annoying noises in controlled environments. They did not test chronic, consistent stress sometimes caused by a strained living situation, financial problems, illness, or long-term problems at work. While acute stresses do exist, the majority of people suffer from long-term, deep-seated stressors over time.

While none of the previous studies found an increase in stomach acid as a result of stress, one interesting study from 1990 found a correlation with stress-induced increases in stomach acid. It found that people with certain personality traits respond differently to stress, and this response either increases or decreases the production of stomach acid. They found that people who are generally laid back, analytically thinking people tend to have decreased stomach acid when exposed to acute stressors. On the contrary, people who are more emotional and quick to react have elevated stomach acid when stress is introduced. This shows again that there is something more going on with stress and acid reflux, yet the causality is still unclear.

To consider another side of the story, we also know that breathing changes as a result of stress. While a calm, resting person will take long, deep breaths, a person under stress will begin to take shallow, short breaths. The response is as old as the human race. In times of acute stress, labeled the "fight or flight" response, early humans would need to increase the oxygen entering the body to prepare for a possible "fight or flight" situation. In response to the stress of possible harm or death, the heart rate quickens, and breathing quickens to supply more oxygen to muscles, including the heart. This is an involuntary body function, so there is no control over it unless you are aware it is occurring and you consciously try to control your breathing.

The unfortunate side effect of shallow breathing is a decrease in strength in the muscles that surround the lower esophageal sphincter. Deep breathing allows these muscles to stretch to their maximum and then contract. Shallow breathing uses only a small amount of muscle capacity to work. It would be like doing a bicep curl at the gym and only flexing the muscle halfway. The whole muscle is not being worked out. Therefore, it weakens over time.

This is an excellent theory to help explain why stress leads to acid reflux. When chronic stress is present, the likelihood of shallow breathing increases. The muscles around the lower esophageal sphincter weaken, leaving the lower esophageal sphincter unsupported and ready to let in unwanted stomach acid.

Bacteria and GERD

Emerging science is beginning to pinpoint the microbiome, a collection of multiple beneficial bacterial strains living in the gut, as a cause of pressure. It is well known that a variety of bacteria called the gastrointestinal system home usually provide several services to the body in exchange for space to live. Bacteria aid in the breakdown and absorption of vitamins and minerals and help regulate the digestive process. Good, non-harmful strains of bacteria in large colonies help to keep smaller colonies of harmful bacteria in check. They act as an extension to the immune system. This is why yogurt is recommended to help digestive issues. The bacteria present in cultured yogurt help increase the colonies of good bacteria living in the gut, therefore aiding in the digestive process and maintaining the populations of harmful bugs.

Bacteria feed on several nutrients, but the most popular is simple sugars broken down from carbohydrate-rich foods like pasta, bread, and fruit. As the bacteria feed on these nutrients, they create gas as a byproduct. The more simple sugars to feed on the more gas the colony will produce. The gases have nowhere to go but up, settling in the stomach, building pressure. When the lower esophageal sphincter opens to relieve some pressure, it lets the opportunistic stomach acid in, reaching and damaging the esophageal lining.

While beneficial bacteria help the body break down food, harmful strains, like Helicobacter pylori (H. Pylori for short), cause more stomach acid to be produced, causing or exacerbating acid reflux symptoms. The human body has a long history of exposure to H. Pylori and therefore knows how to rid itself of it. H. Pylori is sensitive to stomach acid and thrives in a neutral or alkaline environment. Knowing this, the body increases the release of stomach acid in response to the presence of the bacteria. H. Pylori is a tough bug to get rid of, so the stomach acid is raised typically for longer periods, resulting in consistent reflux symptoms. As the stomach cells are exposed to more acid than normal for a long period, peptic ulcers begin to develop. If left untreated, the ulcers bleed, leaking much-needed blood from the body. If persistent, nutrient deficiencies and other significant problems develop through the loss of blood. Not to mention, the condition is very painful. Shooting, stabbing pain is a common complaint. Along with stomach acid-reducing agents, a patient is likely to need antibiotics to help the body fight against H. Pylori infection.

Pregnancy

Acid reflux can be observed in women during their first pregnancy due to the increased pressure from the gradually growing fetus in addition to enhanced levels of hormones. It is at its peak in the third trimester, and the symptoms of acid reflux start fading away soon after delivery.

Smoking

Apart from increasing the danger of esophagus cancer, the following harmful effects of smoking are considered to be responsible for causing acid reflux:

- Enhancement of Acid Secretion
- Reduced Muscle Function of LES
- Reduced Production of Saliva (Saliva is effective in acid neutralization)
- Damaged Mucus Membranes
- Impaired Reflexes of Throat Muscles

Diet

Lying in bed immediately after consuming food or having a larger meal can result in initiating heartburning and various other symptoms of acid reflux, i.e. problems in food swallowing, dry cough, etc. The following everyday foods are known to cause acid reflux:

- Carbonated drinks
- Alcohol
- Spicy foods, e.g. chilies and curries
- Chocolate
- Tea (with Tea Leaves) or Coffee, including both decaffeinated and regular
- Citrus fruits, i.e. lemons, oranges etc.
- Fried or fatty foods
- Onions and Garlic
- Food containing Tomato, e.g. pizza, salsa and spaghetti sauce
- Mint

There are many other reasons for acid reflux including:

- Obesity and overweight
- Eating right before sleeping
- Consuming larger meals and afterward either bending over at the waist or lying in bed
- Consuming muscle relaxants, various BP-controlling medications, and even aspirin or ibuprofen, etc.

Chapter 3: How Food and Symptoms Relate

A combination of lean proteins, comparatively slow low-carbs, and fats can prove to be very pivotal to weight loss, which indeed helps in lowering the risk of having GERD in the first place. Beginners should go for a protein shake for breakfast for an effective and faster approach towards weight loss.

Lowering the intake of foods with higher sugar impact can reduce the risk of GERD. Research also concluded that simple carbs could contribute more to GERD as compared to dietary fats.

Digestive enzymes can be consumed so that fats and proteins are broken down and digested more conveniently in the stomach. Thus symptoms like bloating gas are less likely to happen.

Acidity and Alkalinity

On a pH scale, zero is considered to be acidic while 14 is considered to be entirely alkaline. pH 7 is considered to be neutral. These pH levels vary through our bodies. The pH of our blood ranges between 7.35 and 7.45 and is considered to be slightly alkaline. The alkaline diet is very effective in keeping your blood pH levels maintained.

Breaking Acid-Generation Habits and Establishing Acid-Reduction Practices:

1. Eat Green

Alkaline foods like legumes, fruits, roots, nuts, and veggies should be consumed in abundance. Opt for these foods rather than meats and grains. Go for green or dark vegetables like avocados, beetroot, kale, spinach, etc.

2. Lower Acidic Foods

It's not necessary to completely boycott meats, refined sugars, dairy, and grains, but it is preferred to lower their intake to lower the acidity of your body.

3. Avoid Alcohol Consumption

Alcoholic drinks are known to be high in sugar and extremely acidic. They are not meant to be removed entirely, but their intake should be lowered considerably.

4. Drink Alkaline Water

Water is very vital for our health. It is essential to consume eight to ten glasses of alkaline water daily to have access to a healthy lifestyle. Instead of tap water (pH 6.5 to 7), opt for alkaline water (pH 9) to effectively balance acid-alkaline levels in the body. Its molecules are small and can permeate your body efficiently, keeping you hydrated for a long time.

5. Opt for Natural Energy-Boosting Beverages

Say no to caffeine and sugar-based drinks. Go for natural alkaline drinks, which are known to clean the digestive system, strengthen the metabolism, and balance the acidity in the body.

6. Exercise Properly

Effectively exercise for 30 minutes every day to counter acidity. The sweat provides a different medium for the acidity to leave while helping the blood to alkalize and oxygenate.

7. Avoid Stress

Stress is known for generating high acid levels in the body, so try avoiding it by practicing deep breathing, yoga, or long walks, etc.

Food Allergies, Sensitivities and Intolerance

The difference between food allergy and food intolerance needs to be understood comprehensively.

Actual food allergy is very rare as compared to intolerance. It affects approximately 8% of children, and 4% of adults. It is a quick reaction by the immune system to proteins in certain foods, e.g. nuts and milk, and can be verified easily by a test conducted in a lab. On the other hand, food intolerance is a common reaction and a delayed response to some natural or artificial chemicals in foods involving various foods. There is no certain laboratory-oriented test for this, so it is tested by removing items from a diet one at a time.

Understand your reaction and preferences to food while turning towards the acid reflux diet plan and note the reactions of your body to the meal you are consuming for the effective working of the plan. There are five main versatile categories for food intolerance symptoms, and every family member could have any of them. They include:

- Asthma, running nose, nose and ear infections
- Mouth ulcers, stomach aches, constipation, urinary urgency, diarrhea, etc.
- Eczema, skin rashes, hives, etc.
- Headaches or migraines
- Depression, anxiety, restlessness, etc.

Chapter 4: Acid-Alkaline Balancing

1. Eat Small Meals

Eat small and nutritious. Maintain a ratio of 70–30 percent alkaline to acidic foods.

2. Stop Eating at Least Four Hours before Bedtime

Posture plays a vital role in having the risk of GERD. Always eat three to four hours before sleeping to avoid acid reflux.

3. Wear Loose Clothing

Loose clothing lets your abdomen relax as there is no pressure on it. This can lower down your acid reflux and can be very effective for overweight people.

4. If You Are Overweight, Lose Weight

An increase in weight, no matter how tiny the increment is, means a higher risk of having GERD. Exercise properly to lose weight effectively.

5. Minimize Fat in Foods

Always go for low-fat foods to avoid the risk of GERD. Food categories are explained further in the next chapter.

6. Avoid Foods That May Increase AIP

AIP (autoimmune protocol) is a result of bacterial overgrowth and mal digested carbs. Increased AIP results in GERD. It is recommended to avoid any foods causing AIP.

7. Avoid Foods or Substances That Weaken Your LES

There are numerous causes for the weakening of the lower esophageal sphincter, and almost all of them can be avoided easily. The following are some of them.

8. Overeating or Being Overweight

Overeating or overweight leads to excessive pressure build-up on the LES as the stomach swells. After some time, the LES loses its durability and shape and thus starts allowing acid to reach upwards, which furthers weakens it.

9. Smoking

The chemicals and toxins found in cigarette smoke make the membranes of the LES weak. Smoking also increases the acidity levels of the stomach, thus affecting the LES more than normal stomach fluids do.

10. Alcohol Consumption

Alcohol is known to make the LES weak, and it lowers its ability to close. It allows acid to flow up the LES by relaxing the muscles and thus damages it.

11. Various Medications

Medicines like BP meds, sleeping pills, antibiotics, etc. are known to keep the muscles of the LES relaxed, causing the acid to flow upward and damaging it critically.

12. Certain Foods

We don't recommend trigger foods for people with GERD. High-fat foods also relax the LES muscles and cause it damage.

Chapter 5: The pH Battle

You remember sitting in science class and listening to your teacher discuss alkaline and pH levels. You learned that one end of the scale was basic and the other end acidic—with a fair number of experiments to go along with them.

The human body can also be found on the pH scale in several ways. Each part of your body is on the scale in a different place, with your stomach leaning on the acidic side of the scale and your blood being on the alkaline side of the scale—with your other organs and members being found all across the board.

You will be surprised to learn that when you are struggling with acid reflux, you are dealing with a low amount of acid in your stomach. Many people assume that you get reflux when you have too much acid in your stomach and it creeps through the sphincter, but this isn't always the case.

Your stomach is supposed to be the holding compartment for stomach acid. It's where the acid is created; it's where the acid should be stored and where the food is broken down significantly before it finishes its digestive journey.

When dealing with acid reflux, the acid created in your stomach creeps into your esophagus, resulting in a lower amount of stomach acid. It's no surprise that your body is a system that works with itself in a variety of ways, and when one part of that system is out of balance, the other parts of the body aren't going to work as they should either.

The food you eat affects your body in many ways; many of the foods found on the list of triggers are foods that cause your body to become more acidic as a whole—something you don't want for your acid reflux.

The goal of the acid reflux diet is to eat foods that don't cause your condition to become worse and to incorporate foods that bring your body into balance. As you shop, cook, and eat, look for foods that give your body the desired effect you wish to achieve.

There are dozens of online resources with lists of foods and where they fall on the pH scale. Look into those and base your shopping and cooking on the pH levels of the food you choose to eat. Consult your doctor in regards to what is good for your acid reflux, and ask about the appropriate foods to use.

Don't be afraid to make a list of the foods and the way they affect your body with their pH levels; then get your doctor's opinion on which you should stay away from and which you should choose. As I have said before, your body is going to react uniquely to you. Though there are particular charts and things you can look at that will help with your decisions, you must remember that there is also trial and error involved.

Work with your body to find what works for you, and opt for foods that make you feel your best. This could be the same list as other people you know or you may include foods that only you can eat with your acid reflux. The end goal is to make sure you aren't experiencing acid reflux symptoms. However, if you can make that happen with the foods you are eating, go with that.

The human body is designed much like a machine. The ingested food is the fuel your body needs to function properly.

Too many people settle into the typical diet of fast food and convenience without ever truly considering the long-term effects such things have on the body. When they become ill with any disease, they immediately turn to use medications to manage the symptoms, though they don't do a thing to change their lifestyles.

The more you can learn about the food you are putting into your body and the things that food does to your body, the better off you will be making decisions for your health.

It does take time, and it takes an immense amount of effort, but in the end, it's worth it. No cost can match your health, and though it can be confusing and even frustrating to work with your body until you can get it under control, it's worth it.

Get online now, and search for lists of the pH of the common foods you eat and what those foods do to your body. Search for the kinds of foods that are going to work with your body and alleviate the acid reflux symptoms; then focus on cooking with those foods exclusively.

At the end of this book, you are going to find a few recipes that are essential for your acid reflux and lay the foundation for your cooking in the future.

Chapter 6: Treatment Options

Diagnosing Acid Reflux

Acid reflux is not a serious illness if it only happens once a month, as most individuals may experience it at some points in their lives. It may happen if they go to bed immediately after dinner or stoop down after eating.

When acid reflux symptoms occur more than twice a week, it becomes a GERD or gastroesophageal reflux disease that could lead to complications, even if all treatments have been applied.

Physical examination is needed if there is no lasting relief, even if you have employed lifestyle changes and home remedies. The medical physician will undertake several tests to be in a position to diagnose the real causes of acid reflux and check if there are underlying causes of the discomfort.

Types of Tests for Acid Reflux:

1. Monitoring of pH- The doctor performs this to check the acidity of the esophagus by inserting a device to the patient's esophagus and allowing it to stay for one to two days. This is to determine the pH level of the gut flora in the digestive tract.

2. Endoscopy- The doctor will look inside the patient's esophagus and gastrointestinal tract with the use of an endoscope. The patient has to empty their bowel and refrain from taking solid food several hours before performing the endoscopy. The doctor or surgeon will sedate the patient using general anesthesia to avoid discomfort.

3. Barium swallow- Before performing this test, the doctor will let the patient swallow a barium sulfate solution to have a vivid X-ray examination of the upper gastrointestinal tract. This is to check if the patient has a narrow esophagus or stomach problems. The barium sulfate is combined with water and, once ingested by the patient, it coats the intestinal walls and lining of the stomach to allow for a clearer picture of what is happening inside.

4. Biopsy- This is to check the tissue samples taken from the gastrointestinal tract and esophagus while performing an endoscopy. The doctor will check the specimen using a microscope to look for possible anatomical abnormalities and infection inside the body.

5. Esophageal manometry- This test is used to measure the muscle coordination and the strength of the esophagus when the patient is swallowing food. A tube is inserted into the nose that will pass down through the throat, and then to the esophagus, and lastly into the stomach. Manometry is performed on patients who have symptoms of acid reflux or heartburn by observing the peristalsis of the esophagus.

Peristalsis is the movement of the muscles in the esophagus, particularly the esophageal sphincter, which is a muscular valve that opens when the food passes and closes to discourage the food and the stomach acid from moving out of the stomach and then going up to the esophagus. Pregnant women and individuals with lung, heart, and other chronic ailments should inform their doctor before undergoing an esophageal manometry.

6. Esophageal impedance-pH monitoring- This outpatient test is performed to measure the non-acid reflux and acidity of the stomach contents by placing sensors in the

esophagus. The patient wears a data recorder by which the symptomatic episodes are recorded for analysis to find out if it is related to the reflux episodes. This test is performed usually within 24 hours. The patient is advised to empty their bowel and avoid eating or drinking four hours before the test.

When to Seek Medical Help

Sufferers of GERD, heartburn, or acid reflux should seek professional help if the medications and home remedies are ineffective. It signals that a specialist in gastroenterology should check your medical condition to have the right treatment administered and prevent complications.

It is time to seek medical help if you have any of the following:

- If you have chest pain
- If you are experiencing shortness of breath
- Pain that reaches the arm and jaw
- If the bleeding and pain persist
- If your voice is hoarse
- If you have difficulty swallowing your food
- If the symptoms of heartburn occur more than twice a week
- If the medications and prevention techniques are ineffective
- If you have lost your voice

Preparing for an Appointment:

Acid reflux is not dangerous initially, but when it develops into a gastroesophageal reflux disease, complications may arise. When the symptoms continue after taking antacids and proton-pump inhibitors (PPIs), you must seek professional help. Be prepared to answer and ask questions from your doctor. Use the FAQs below as a reference when consulting your doctor.

Here are some frequently asked questions (FAQ) by patients:

1. What are the possible causes of acid reflux?

2. Are there other ailments that may have caused my condition?

3. What are the tests needed to diagnose my condition?

4. Which test is best for my age and my existing health condition?

5. What medications should I take?

6. Are these medications safe for my health?

7. What are the complications if I do not take oral medications?

8. What are the side effects of taking anti-reflux medications?

9. What is the right treatment other than taking medications?

10. Is surgery suitable for my age?

11. What causes relapse or recurrence of GERD after an operation?

12. I am pregnant, what treatment is best for my condition?

13. How much is the cost of surgery?

14. What is the best diet for me?

FAQs a health professional may ask:

- How many times do the symptoms occur in a week?
- Is it accompanied by bleeding and burning pain?
- Do you smoke?
- Do you eat a high-fiber diet?
- Are your meals spicy and fatty?
- Do you have chest pain?
- Does the pain reach the arm, jaw, and shoulders?
- Do you lie down or exercise after eating?
- Do you have difficulty swallowing your food?
- What medications are you taking?

Health professionals to look for:

- Gastroenterologist
- Internist
- Family medicine doctor
- Surgeon
- Nurse
- Nursing assistant
- Pharmacist

The muscles found in the lower part of the esophageal sphincter usually open to allow the food to pass from the throat down to the stomach and automatically close to discourage the stomach acids from slipping into the esophagus. When the function of the esophageal sphincter becomes abnormal because of underlying issues, the acid from the stomach will slide up into the esophageal lining and the throat, which release a sour and bitter-tasting fluid.

In some people, the acids are so prevalent that they are hardly able to breathe for a few seconds. The pain can be felt in the lower part of the chest area, and this is where heartburn takes place. Cases of acid reflux can lead to heartburn, or if there is heartburn accompanied by shortness of breath and chest pain, it may signal another disease that should not be overlooked by the sufferer.

Prevention & Treatment for Acid Reflux

There are many ways to prevent acid reflux and gastroesophageal reflux disease that sufferers can employ. Lifestyle factors can contribute to the progression of acid reflux to become a full-blown gastroesophageal reflux disease (GERD) that will ultimately lead to complications and even cancer. Prevention is essential to avoid this condition; included is a lifestyle change. Obesity and smoking are said to be the primary causes of acid reflux and need to be countered at its onset.

Tips for preventing acid reflux:

- Try to lose weight by controlling your diet with proper exercise
- Stop smoking
- Increase your intake of high-fiber foods
- Do not sleep right after taking your meals

- Minimize eating salty, fatty, and spicy foods
- Keep a diary or journal to trace its causes
- Avoid drinking alcoholic, caffeinated, and carbonated drinks
- Eat small but frequent meals
- Refrain from exercises that require you to sit up or bend after a meal
- Add more pillows to elevate your head
- Sleep in a chair when having a daytime nap
- Avoid wearing tight jeans, belts, and clothes
- Refer to your doctor if you are taking other medications that might trigger the acid reflux symptoms

Medications for Acid Reflux:

There are many medications that patients can take to relieve the symptoms of acid reflux, and most of them do not need a doctor's prescription. These medications include proton-pump inhibitors or PPIs and antacids to reduce stomach acidity, and ibuprofen to remove the burning pain caused by heartburn and GERD.

Proton-Pump Inhibitors and Acid Reflux:

Acid reflux is a treatable disease but may develop into a complicated illness, such as cancer. At the onset of this condition, the sufferer may choose to take proton-pump inhibitors or PPIs. PPIs are drugs that help reduce acid production in the stomach to prevent ulcers, hyperacidity, gastritis, and acid reflux. PPIs block the enzymes in the intestinal wall where the acid is produced.

Acid is the primary agent in developing ulceration and scarring in the gastrointestinal tract and esophagus. Long-term use of proton-pump inhibitor medications should be stopped if the symptoms of acid reflux persist as they can cause organ damage, block the absorption of nutrients, and lead to risk of infection, among other side effects. The PPIs can be bought as over-the-counter medication and have been commercially available for more than two decades now.

List of Proton-Pump Inhibitors (PPIs):

1. Protonix (pantoprazole)- It is prescribed as a treatment for esophagitis and Zollinger-Ellison syndrome and acid reflux because it can reduce stomach acid. Patients with a history of allergies in certain medications, such as pantoprazole and benzimidazole, as well as illnesses such as liver disease, osteoporosis, osteopenia and low magnesium in the blood should ask their doctor for advice.

2. Aciphex (rabeprazole)- This oral medication is used to reduce the level of stomach acidity that causes acid reflux and GERD. It is also used to heal duodenal and esophageal ulcers, Zollinger-Ellison syndrome, and H. pylori infections. It can be taken both on an empty or filled stomach.

3. Nexium (esomeprazole)- This PPI helps reduce the amount of stomach acid to treat gastroesophageal reflux disease or acid reflux, Zollinger-Ellison syndrome, and erosive esophagitis and prevent bleeding in the esophagus. It can be taken orally or injected when the patient cannot take it by mouth.

4. Prevacid (lansoprazole)- It reduces acid production in the stomach and treats erosive esophagitis and intestinal ulcers.

5. Dexilant (dexlansoprazole)- This oral medication is used to treat acid reflux and GERD and prevents esophageal

ulcers and bleeding by reducing the amount of acid in the stomach. Consult a doctor if symptoms of GERD persist even after long-term use.

6. Egerid (immediate-release omeprazole with sodium bicarbonate).

7. Prilosec & Zegerid (omeprazole)- It is prescribed by a gastroenterologist to reduce stomach acid and treat GERD and erosive esophagitis. Patients with gastric ulcer caused by H. pylori infection can take omeprazole along with antibiotics.

Antacids and Gastric Reflux:

People who are prone to have dyspepsia, hyperacidity, and acid reflux can also take antacids to neutralize stomach acid triggered by missed meals and drinking alcoholic beverages. They can buy antacids without a doctor's prescription as they are commercially available in chewable tablets, chewing gum, dissolving tablets, and liquid forms from pharmacies. They are taken to alleviate the pain and acidity by reacting with the contents of the stomach and not directly on the cells that produce acids in the duodenal lining.

Antacids are composed of various compounds that include magnesium hydrochloride, aluminum, sodium bicarbonate, and calcium carbonate. Although antacids are generally safe to use for pregnant and lactating women, they are not recommended for children who are 12 years old and below or for patients with kidney disease. Mild cases of acid reflux and GERD can be remedied with antacids, but taking them for more than two weeks is not advisable.

Types of Antacids:

- Calcium carbonate - They come with brand names Tums and Rolaids and promote absorption of calcium in the body.

- Aluminum hydroxide & magnesium carbonate - They come with the brand name Gaviscon, which is composed of alginic acid and a foaming agent. The top of the stomach contents will be coated with the antacid to prevent the acid from making direct contact with the esophagus. The alginate is derived from brown algae.
- Aluminum hydroxide & magnesium hydroxide - They come with brand names Maalox and Mylanta and contain simethicone, which is responsible for breaking down the air inside the stomach. Flatulence and burping are reduced after taking this medication.

Other Medications and Acid Reflux:

There are certain medications to treat other ailments that can trigger the symptoms of acid reflux. Among them are pain killers, antidepressants, antibiotics, nitroglycerin, and drugs for the treatment of anxiety, hypertension, and osteoporosis.

We understand that if you have hypertension and psychosomatic illness, stopping their medication can make your existing condition worse. If you want to remove the discomfort of acid reflux, you have to inform your doctor about your other drugs to avoid contraindications and side effects. You may still have to take all your medications on a specific schedule. Here are some facts on how to address this problem:

- Read the medical literature and check the instructions carefully.
- You should be aware that certain drugs are to be taken before or after meals.
- Not following the instructions can only worsen your health condition.

- Do not exceed your doctor's recommendations.
- Follow the schedule of all your medications and do not double-dose for a missed schedule.
- Avoid self-medication to treat acid reflux, especially if you have another illness.
- Post your doctor's prescription and schedule of medications on a corkboard.

Reminders When Taking Medications:

Note that antacids should not be taken in combination with proton-pump inhibitors or taken within one hour of each other as the antacid can slow down the function of PPIs. Although PPIs are prescribed to block the acid in the stomach, overdosage may cause the stomach to produce less acid.

In his editorial, San Francisco Department of Public Health chief Mitchell Katz pointed out that PPIs do not at all guarantee to treat GERD, heartburn, and acid reflux because their functions are only limited in the treatment of bleeding ulcers, Zollinger-Ellison syndrome, and a severe case of acid reflux.

Katz added that the dependence of PPIs would decrease the body's natural ability to block the H. pylori bacteria because the stomach acid is depleted. Stomach acid serves as a blocking force against bacterial infection that may cause food poisoning. PPIs can trigger bone loss, hip fracture, and pulmonary infection.

Melatonin and Acid Reflux:

Melatonin is an indole that is said to cause sleep. It plays a significant role in stimulating the activity of the lower esophageal sphincter so that stomach contents will not back up into the esophagus. This conclusion is based on animal studies as reported by the Life Extension Foundation.

Melatonin has been proven effective in healing sores and ulcers in the digestive tract. Its presence in the GI tract through the enterochromaffin cells can prevent and cure irritable bowel syndrome, stomach upset, and dyspepsia. Taking melatonin along with natural food supplements is more effective than proton-pump inhibitors, particularly omeprazole.

Chapter 7: Natural Remedies for Acid Reflux, LPR and GERD

Organic Honey, Fresh Basil, Holy Basil Tea, and Indian Gooseberry

Some of the natural GERD remedies I am going to talk about are natural and holistic food and herbal therapies. One is unrefined organic honey, which is cheap, simple, and available to try, and it helps reduce burning. The honey helps the pH, and a little bit at bedtime may calm down the burning.

Another is fresh basil, which is an Ayurvedic remedy to relieve acid reflux; some people chew on the fresh basil leaves, but you can buy holy basil tea at the health food store or tulsi tea, which is very good for calming the system and Indian gooseberry is an herb that helps the digestive tract against stomach acid.

Licorice Root, Bromelain, and Slippery Elm

Another one is licorice root, which soothes as it builds up a little protective layer of mucus in the esophagus, and you can get it as a tea; watch your blood pressure, as it can occasionally go up. Also, deglycyrrhized licorice, which you can get as a tablet, is soothing and calming. Bromelain is an enzyme in pineapple, so taking this enzyme or even eating some pineapple before meals is a way to help digest food. It helps move the food through faster so it's not sitting in there forever.

Slippery elm is another thing that coats the stomach like gooseberry that you can buy and try. So, if you go to the health food store, you may find these things, or some combination may help you tremendously—try one at a time and see what effect it has on your system and acid reflux symptoms. Even if you have no symptoms, take heed of this point—things that aid your digestion are helping you stay healthier and younger longer!

Cayenne Pepper, Apple Cider Vinegar, and Baking Soda

Apple cider vinegar and cayenne pepper—now, it's not intuitive, but some people use cayenned pepper. This is a hot burning pepper, and once you put it in water, it seems like it might burn. But some people have used this to heal inflammation and their ulcers, the same thing with the apple cider vinegar, organic vinegar; you put a little bit in the water, and you think it would burn, but it helps digest food and move it through.

Again, you get more nutrients out of the food you eat. The apple cider vinegar may be the easiest ultimate solution! Use an ounce or so before or after meals, especially if you have symptoms of heartburn and watch them fade away! And the bonus is that for older people, it is adding an acid to your digestive system, letting you get more nutrients into your system that you need, like B12, calcium, and magnesium. This may help you avoid bone problems and mental decline.

In a pinch for quick relief, you can use baking soda, the yellow box and not the powder. But a note to add here is that baking soda is an antacid, and if we have low stomach production of acid as we grow older, perhaps it is better to add an acidic element to help our digestion like the apple cider vinegar so that we get more nourishment from the foods we do eat. However, baking soda in a pinch can soothe heartburn.

Eat Slowly and Smaller Meals

A big thing everyone can do is chew their food slowly. If you eat it slowly, and you chew it up, you're going to digest part of it with the enzymes in your mouth. So, when it goes down, it will be easier to move through the stomach and get started, digesting it faster.

And avoid large, greasy, fatty food meals; slow down, take your time, eat smaller meals, eat slower, and then you will be less likely to have acid reflux.

Digestive Enzymes

Another thing to use, especially if you are on the road, is digestive enzymes. They work similarly to apple cider vinegar. Digestive enzymes are fabulous; I see a lot of people that they help. All our foods these days are cooked or microwaved (I suggest you throw out your microwave or only use it in an emergency).

You could use some raw enzymes; as we grow older, we lose the ability to digest our food, so if you take digestive enzymes as a supplement, this will help in many ways. There are a lot of great digestive enzyme products on the market, and these are very helpful—you can take them as capsules.

Finally, you can eat some raw fruits and vegetables. I have had people tell me they'll have a little pineapple, small papaya, a little bit of fresh apple; chew that up and eat it slowly before your meal, so then you get the enzymes in there to help digest the food and move it through. That's pretty simple and cheap, and you can't get much more natural than that!

Probiotics

Another important thing is if you do not have regular bowel movements, everything is going to back up and cause the stomach to empty slower. To help this, probiotics are fantastic, and I think everyone should be on them; we need to keep those good gut bacteria down in the stomach.

If you're drinking tap water with chlorine, the chlorine is killing them off, everything in the gut, and if you're not eating fermented food that has got the good bacteria in it, then you are not replacing it, and probiotics are the answer.

You can get them as 25 or 50 billion in a little capsule, and I love the chewables because you start right in the mouth getting the bacteria in. Yogurt, kefir, sauerkraut—all those things help keep the good bacteria count high, and I think that health begins in the gut; it is so essential for our mental health as your mood can be affected.

Why, there are all kinds of studies showing that if you are depressed, or anxious, taking probiotics can be an excellent start to improving that! Again, I love the chewables, but anyway, it is good if you can get them in.

No GERD Supplement

Amongst other supplements that I have used, there is one that is called "No GERD." It is a simple formula, and it uses d-limonene, which is an organic compound and includes certain citrus fruits. So, the secret is in the rind, and orange peels have it.

These are called terpenes. The terpenes are any one of a class of unsaturated hydrocarbons, such as the carotenes, found in the essential oils of many plants. This helps to improve heartburn and acidity, so this is one of the things I have used to transition people off the drugs.

I start them off at a bigger dose, maybe twice a day, of the No GERD and taper down the PPI and H2 blocker so that it will prevent that sudden acid reflux rebound, and they can use this as a replacement to help get them off it and then switch to more natural methods.

Here is more on the No GERD formula, which can be used to wean patients off PPIs and H2 Blockers.

Gastro Mend

Gastro Mend—another one I use is from "Designs for Health," which is a perfect vitamin company, and this one is a combination of several different things that I've used for stomach acid and heartburn. I've had several people cured of H. pylori without taking an antibiotic, and H. pylori is a difficult bacteria to heal in the stomach.

I've seen many people healed by Gastro Mend. It's got mastic gum in it, and this has been used for thousands of years in the Middle East and Greece, it is a plant, a gum that helps. It also has MSM in it, deglycerized licorice, and zinc carnosine, which soothes, coats and heals, and blocks the H. pylori. I've seen great results with that.

DoTERRA Essential Oil

Another thing is doTERRA, the Essential Oils company sells it as an oil or in a capsule, so it is easy to chew. It is a combination of several things, ginger, pepper, tarragon, fennel, caraway, anise, and coriander, and essential oils.

All of these have been used individually for intestinal problems, but in a combination and in a little pill it is very easy to soothe heartburn, and you can swallow it as it helps soothe and calm the stomach effectively. Again, there are no reported side effects with this product either.

Chapter 8: Cleansing and Detoxification

1. Consuming Lots of Cleansing Foods

Cleansing our body from the impurities that deposit deep in many parts of our body is the main step for curing our heartburn. We eat many kinds of food materials, and some of them have impurities that are not easily removable. We also intake a large number of impurities through our nostrils. So, cleansing is the best way to get rid of many impurities presenting inside our body. One of the main parts of our digestive system is the colon, which is a five to six-foot-long muscular tube that absorbs fluids and some nutrients. Any harmful effect on our colon directly impacts our digestive system thereby causing heartburn in many cases. So, our primary purpose of cleansing is to clean our colon from impurities. Now, there are a variety of foods that are helpful in cleansing our colon and keeping it functioning properly.

Some of the helpful foods to cleanse your colon: --

1. Raw green vegetables: -- Raw green vegetables are a must in your diet if you are looking to cure heartburn. However, the most beneficial part of fresh green vegetables is that they are helpful in cleansing your colon. Our digestive system works in a precise way, i.e. the digestive enzymes of our digestive system amalgamate with the digestive enzymes of food to break it down thoroughly. But as we become older, the ability of our digestive system diminishes and so the number of digestive enzymes inside our stomach decreases. This is the main reason why heartburn is a common disease among older people. Cooking food at a higher temperature destroys the natural digestive enzymes of our food, and that's why raw green vegetables are mandatory when you want to cure your heartburn problem because then you can retain the natural

enzymes of food and digest the food properly while eating it raw.

2. Foods containing fiber: -- I have already mentioned the benefits of fiber-rich food in the earlier section of this book. Now I am emphasizing fiber-rich food again because it is also beneficial for the cleansing of your colon. Both soluble and insoluble fibers add bulk that gently stretches and stimulates the intestinal lining, ensuring healthy rhythmic muscular contractions that are helpful in moving the food through your digestive tract. This rhythmic movement is also beneficial in preventing constipation. So, include lots of fiber in your food to cleanse your colon.

3. Probiotic foods: -- Do you know what probiotic foods are? Probiotic foods are foods that contain a reasonable amount of some of the natural and healthy bacteria that live in our colon. These bacteria accelerate our digestion process and keep our colon healthy. Some of the probiotic foods such as yogurt, kimchi, and miso many species of beneficial bacteria like bifidus and lactobacillus. You will also get "inulin" that are being used by these bacteria as a food source like beans, flaxseed, apples, and asparagus.

2. Cleansing Your Liver

Cleansing our blood is as vital as cleansing other parts of our body. But our liver needs special cleansing because it is one of the most crucial parts of the human body. The liver can filter the blood from the digestive tract before heading to other body parts. The liver also produces some essential proteins, detoxifying chemicals, and metabolizing drugs. Before you go for a liver cleansing diet, get a thorough check-up for your liver, and consult your dietician and take some suggestions for how to start your diet program. If you have any allergies, then avoid consuming the food that causes your allergies.

Here are some of the tips before beginning a liver cleanse diet: --

1. Don't follow the diet if you are pregnant, nursing, have any cancer, or you have any liver disease or hepatitis.

2. Drink two large glasses of water on an empty stomach every morning after you wake up. Add some juice or fresh lemon if you want. It will be more prudent to use a green smoothie recipe containing raw vegetables. (Use any recipe from our list)

3. Avoid grains containing gluten, especially wheat.

4. If you are on a diet and don't want to ingest any heavy protein foods, then you can use a protein powder smoothie. (You can add a scoop of whey protein or any other protein of your choice in our smoothie recipes)

5. The primary purpose of cleansing your liver is to remove the impurities from your body. If you buy traditional food from the market, you won't fulfill your primary motivation. So, I would suggest you use organic food for your liver cleanse. Organic foods are a bit expensive, but you can use them during your liver cleanse program for maximum results.

Here are some common foods that help cleanse your liver: --

1. Beetroots and carrots

2. Green leafy vegetables

3. Avocados

4. Apples

5. Olive oil

The best way to consume liver-cleansing foods is to make smoothies. Smoothies are a combination of one or more liver-cleansing food with natural sweeteners. All you have to do is find the best combination of the above-described foods that taste best. Mix them and take them in the morning. One more thing, you must drink two glasses of water every morning on an empty stomach.

Chapter 9: The Acid Reflux Diet

Several studies and research have been undertaken on acid reflux and GERD. Virtually every one of them points out that a poor diet made up mostly of processed foods serves as a contributing factor to the development of the disease. There is also the fact that it is easy for anyone to eat a lot of processed foods.

Overeating and forgetting mindful eating practices are some of the things that can aggravate your stomach, which may result in acid reflux. Everyone's gut differs from each other, and each one reacts to different foods differently. However, people have common sensitivities to foods that seem to trigger heartburn.

Knowing these triggers and cutting them out of your diet is one of the essential things you need to do. For relief from pain and excellent overall digestive health, you need the best acid reflux diet along with taking critical steps in breaking your unpleasant eating habits. Diet, along with some changes in your lifestyle, can be as effective as medicines in relieving heartburn symptoms.

As often as you can, add GMO-free organic foods. Additionally, your diet should include foods meant to increase your organic food intake. You should also take probiotic-rich foods and supplements that support the growth of healthy bacteria. Besides that, your diet must have reduced grains but high-quality protein, which helps protect your digestive tract.

These changes to your diet can reduce your risk factors for obesity, inflammation, and other complications related to severe chronic diseases. In this book, you will discover the best foods to include in your diet to treat your symptoms.

30-Day Meal Plan

Day 1:

Breakfast: Quinoa Porridge

Lunch: Potato Medley Soup

Dinner: Baked Herb Tilapia

Day 2:

Breakfast: Banana Bread

Lunch: Crab Cakes with Healthy Tartar Sauce

Dinner: Simple Vegetable Broth

Day 3:

Breakfast: Vegetable Tacos

Lunch: Halibut and Veggie Packets

Dinner: Roast Rib of Beef

Day 4:

Breakfast: Apricot Oats

Lunch: Vegetable Soup

Dinner: Fish Tacos with Guacamole

Day 5:

Breakfast: Ginger and Banana Smoothies

Lunch: Chicken Noodle Soup

Dinner: Zucchini and Carrot Frittata

Day 6:

Breakfast: Banana and Mango Smoothie

Lunch: Miso Soup with Tofu and Greens

Dinner: Tilapia with Cantaloupe Salsa

Day 7:

Breakfast: Sweet Potato Tarts

Lunch: Coconut Panko Shrimp

Dinner: Broccoli and Cheese Baked Potato

Day 8:

Breakfast: Sweet Potato Toast with Almond Butter

Lunch: Baked Chicken Tenders

Dinner: Miso-Glazed Scallops

Day 9:

Breakfast: Chia Seeds Pudding

Lunch: Vegetable Beef Soup

Dinner: Salmon and Lentils

Day 10:

Breakfast: Chicken with Fennel Turmeric

Lunch: Asian Veggie and Tofu

Dinner: Pho with Zucchini Noodles

Day 11:

Breakfast: English Muffins

Lunch: Chicken Noodle Soup

Dinner: Maple-Glazed Salmon

Day 12:

Breakfast: Poached Eggs Spinach

Lunch: Fisherman's Stew

Dinner: Turkey Meatloaf Muffins

Day 13:

Breakfast: Muesli-Style Oatmeal

Lunch: Cream of Broccoli Soup

Dinner: Turkey Meatballs

Day 14:

Breakfast: Banana-Flax Smoothie

Lunch: One-Pot Chicken Stew

Dinner: Sirloin Steak Salad with Papaya Vinaigrette

Day 15:

Breakfast: Sweet Melon Smoothie

Lunch: Creamy Pumpkin Soup

Dinner: Breaded Crispy Shrimp

Day 16:

Breakfast: Green Aloe Vera Smoothie

Lunch: Cream of Broccoli Soup

Dinner: Vegetable and Tofu Rice

Day 17:

Breakfast: Chia Breakfast Pudding with Cantaloupe

Lunch: Hamburger Stew

Dinner: Steamer Clams with Fennel

Day 18:

Breakfast: Fruit and Yogurt Parfait

Lunch: Italian Vegetable Soup

Dinner: Shrimp and Grits

Day 19:

Breakfast: Maple-Ginger Oatmeal

Lunch: Patty Melt Soup

Dinner: Inside-Out Cabbage Rolls

Day 20:

Breakfast: Corn Porridge with Maple and Raisins

Lunch: Easy Tuna Melt

Dinner: Herb-Crusted Lamb Chops

Day 21:

Breakfast: Milky Oats

Lunch: Broiled Shrimp

Dinner: Open-Faced Stuffed Burgers

Day 22:

Breakfast: Coconut Quinoa

Lunch: Sweet Potato and Corn Stew

Dinner: Herb and Sour Cream Baked Halibut

Day 23:

Breakfast: Chia Quinoa

Lunch: Cream of Broccoli Soup

Dinner: Flank Steak with Chimichurri

Day 24:

Breakfast: Breakfast Muesli

Lunch: Kale and Herb-Stuffed Turkey Cutlets

Dinner: Spaghetti with Watercress and Pea Pesto

Day 25:

Breakfast: Fast Porridge

Lunch: Beef Tacos

Dinner: Turkey and Spinach Rollatini

Day 26:

Breakfast: Chia Breakfast

Lunch: Roasted Lamb Chops with Chimichurri

Dinner: Lentil Tacos

Day 27:

Breakfast: Watermelon Salad

Lunch: Easy Turkey Burgers

Dinner: White Bean, Chicken, and Rosemary Casserole

Day 28:

Breakfast: Banana Shake

Lunch: Ground Lamb and Lentils

Dinner: Zucchini Ribbons with Parmesan Cream Sauce

Day 29:

Breakfast: Delicious Avocado Smoothie

Lunch: Broiled Shrimp

Dinner: Hamburger Stroganoff with Zucchini Noodles

Day 30:

Breakfast: Layered Oats

Lunch: Shepherd's Pie Muffins

Dinner: Oven-baked Chicken

Chapter 10: Food List - What to Eat and What to Avoid

Foods Not to Eat:

The following foods are known to make GERD worse and tend to be acidic. Their intake should be lowered and reduced very much.

- Foods that have High Fats and Oil (these foods may result in the relaxation of the sphincter in the stomach)
- Fatty Meats (they are highly acidic while having a higher amount of fatty acids and cholesterol levels)
- Foods that are the sources of Saturated Fats. These include full-fat cheese (highly acidic) and whole milk
- Excessive amounts of Salt
- Mint
- Chocolate
- Carbonated Beverages (sodas)
- Caffeine
- Acidic drinks, which include coffee and orange juice, etc.
- Acidic foods, which include tomato sauce, etc.

Foods to Eat:

The following foods are known to be alkaline and can be used to avoid the risk of having GERD. These foods should be consumed in abundance.

- Carbs present in various veggies, low-acid fruits, and certain whole grains
- Proteins from trout, lentils, lean poultry (without skin), salmon, and beans, which are low in cholesterol levels.
- Foods rich in Vitamin C content, e.g. veggies and low-acid fruits
- Green Vegetables like spinach, asparagus, Brussels sprouts, broccoli, and kale, etc.
- High-Fiber food, especially high in soluble fiber foods, is known to lower the risk of GERD.
- High-Fiber Fruits (rich in potassium and magnesium) like apples, melons, avocados, bananas, peaches, pears, and berries, etc.
- Eggs (irrespective of their cholesterol levels)
- Avoid foods or substances that Increase Acidity
- Straightforwardly lower the intake of acidic foods like Meat and Grains, etc.
- Eat more Alkaline Foods
- Consume more Veggies and Fruits like broccoli, spinach, bananas, etc.

Chapter 11: Important Herbs to Embrace

There are a wide variety of herbs and supplements that you can take to help reduce your acid reflux symptoms, and, in some cases, long-term exposure may well help to cure acid reflux. For example, ginger helps the stomach to evacuate food faster, which, in turn, aids digestion and L-glutamine is an amino acid that helps to repair damage to the stomach and intestinal lining, which again over time might help to cure acid reflux.

The material that follows is quite varied, and it covers herbs and supplements for stomach and intestinal health and not just acid reflux. Experiment and see which ones work well for you!

Ginger

Ginger is a popular food supplement, but also it is a wondrous herb that has many excellent traits, one of which is aiding digestion. In a clinical study on the effectiveness of ginger on speeding up the breakdown of food in the stomach, they took 24 participants and gave them 1.2 grams of ginger one hour before eating a meal and then observed how long it took for the food to transit from the stomach into the intestines. Usually, it takes approximately 20 minutes for the food to transit. However, the average figure that came back in this group was a transit time of only 13 minutes. This indicates that the ginger helped the food predigest approximately 50% faster than normal. What this suggests is that ginger will help food to predigest, which will, in turn, make for better chyme and thus an easier time on the intestines when it comes to absorbing the food.

Furthermore, ginger also helps relieve symptoms of nausea. In another clinical trial on 32 pregnant ladies, who were suffering from morning sickness, they were given one gram of ginger per day, and by the end of study 28 out of the 32 women noticed a significant reduction in morning sickness symptoms!

So, ginger not only helps to break down the food but it also helps to settle the stomach, in cases of people who are prone to stomach upset!

There are lots of ways to take ginger. You can add ginger into your cooking, but a very effective and tasty way to take ginger is as a tea.

Ginger Tea

1. Take 250 ml of water (eight ounces) and add in several slices of ginger, taken directly from ginger root. Take some ginger root (about three grams per cup) and peel off the outer layer of skin from one part of it and then cut off several slices. Take these slices and either crush slightly or blend in a mix for a few seconds before adding into the water. Another approach is to pound them slightly in pewter, as once the ginger is crushed a little, its helpful compounds will be released.

2. Boil the water and leave to simmer for a good 10 to 15 minutes to get the essence of the ginger out. When we think about boiling vegetables versus steaming, steaming is always recommended because boiling takes out the nutrients from the vegetables and puts them into the water, whereas steaming does not do this. However, in this case, we want the nutrients within the ginger to come out into the water as we are going to drink it!

3. You will know the tea is ready when a distinct ginger aroma is smelt.

4. Put a tablespoon of honey into a cup.

5. Take one small lemon or half a medium-sized lemon and squeeze into the same cup.

6. Strain the boiled ginger water into the cup containing the honey and lemon. If you have done a good job, the tea

should be strong enough to sting your throat a little bit. This means that you have got the essence of ginger with all of its amazing benefits!

7. Other options include adding in cardamom, which will not only add flavor but also enormous nutritional benefits.

Wheatgrass

Wheatgrass is an awesome yet underrated herb that can help gut health. Wheatgrass is the grass that becomes wheat, being chopped when the grass is only six inches in height. Anyway, this grass possesses many amazing benefits, which include the following benefits:

- Balances the body's pH levels
- Deoxygenates our bodies
- Protects against cancer
- Boosts red blood cell count
- Cleanses the blood
- Detoxifies the liver
- Improves digestion
- Extremely high in nutrients including vitamins A, B6, C, K and E, manganese, selenium, copper and zinc
- Very high in dietary fiber
- Stimulates the thyroid
- Promotes weight loss
- Strengthens bones

- Regulates blood sugar levels
- Improves blood lipid levels
- Increases athletic performance

Wheatgrass is so potent that it's worth taking as a significant health booster and everyone should take it for a couple of reasons. First of all, our diet is very acidic these days, as foods such as milk and dairy products are all acidic. Most foods that are bases are vegetables, so unless you are eating a truckload of vegetables, your body is probably going to be too acidic. Our bodies are meant to operate slightly into the base range of around 7.35–7.45. The pH Scale goes from 0 to 6, which is most acidic to least acidic, with Coke and coffee being around 4 on this scale, and then we have water which is pH neutral, which is 7, and then we go from 8, which is the least base, to 14, which is the most base. So our bodies are meant to be slightly base. Our bloodstream has to maintain this narrow range of 7.35 to 7.45, and to maintain this level our body will even bleach minerals out of our bones to maintain this narrow range in our bloodstream!

Now, aside from imminent death, which would happen if our bloodstream's pH levels ran outside of this narrow range, even when our body manages to artificially maintain this blood level balance, the body, in general, is too acidic, and in extreme cases this can result in acidosis, where a variety of complaints can arise, which include:

- Fatigue
- Drowsiness
- Shortness of breath
- Headaches
- Confusion
- Tremors

If you experience a number of these symptoms, then the chances are that you either have acidosis or are on the way there. Few people develop full-blown acidosis, but lots of people suffer from borderline acidosis whereby they have aches and pains, feel fatigued and drained, and generally their bodies are not working well.

So, how does it relate to gut issues?

Well, while the gut pH level has to be acidic, the body, in general, should be base to function efficiently. For example, an acidic environment promotes fungal growth, bacterial growth, and viral growth within the body. When we get our pH levels back into the normal range, this bodily environment isn't suitable for funguses, bacteria, or viruses. So, getting rid of these pathogenic invaders helps, amongst other things, to maintain a healthy gut. The great thing with wheatgrass is that it helps to get the pH levels back in line without resorting to eating large quantities of vegetables each day.

Also wheatgrass is high in fructans, which promote lactobacilli (healthy gut bacteria that aid digestion and help to kill off nasty funguses such as candida, for example), and they also help promote reabsorption of calcium, which promotes bones health, lowers triglyceride levels, aids heart health and helps to reduce blood glucose levels.

Another great benefit of wheatgrass is its high micronutrient level, which promotes, once again, digestive health, and finally wheatgrass is very high in soluble fiber, to the degree that ingesting wheatgrass can promote bowel movements, especially in people who are having gut health issues.

Wheatgrass is a great herb and will boost your health in general, but yes, it has a great influence on gut health when you initially take wheatgrass. Usually, it will have a strong effect on bowel movements. So, when you start taking wheatgrass at first, don't be surprised if you end up suddenly having to go to the toilet. Fortunately, this will correct itself within a few days or weeks. The good news, however, is that it's your gut righting itself and the reason why there are so many bowel movements is that the wheatgrass is moving stubborn blockages within the intestines. So, as this "crap" (literally) gets thrown out of our bodies, which is good for health and most people who have gut health issues, nearly always there will be a backlog, so moving this backlog is the first step towards good gut health. Also, for people who are suffering from diarrhea, wheatgrass will help to balance the healthy gut bacteria, which will have the reverse effect of normalizing bowel movements!

Regarding how to take wheatgrass, ideally you should grow your own, but this tends to be a big hassle, so while the organic, made at home in your garden wheatgrass is the best, the powder form, which you can get in your local health store, is still pretty good and well worth your while to take it.

To take wheatgrass in powder form, take two tablespoons (30 grams) of it and add in around 250 ml (eight ounces) of water, stir with a spoon and drink. If you have been having lots of stomach health issues, then take this three times a day initially, but when things settle down, take just once a day, as this is enough to promote your gut health and your health in general!

Apple Cider Vinegar

Apple cider vinegar (ACV) goes hand in hand with wheatgrass in that it is a powerful general health elixir, and also it is perfect for gut health. The benefits of ACV include the following:

- Balances the body's pH levels
- Promotes digestion and stomach health
- Aids blood circulation
- Aids weight loss

- Good for heart health
- Relieves joint pain
- Anti-cancerous

Now, out of all these great effects from gut health, we are interested in ACV because of its pH balancing effects and also because of its impact on restoring stomach health.

There are two factors worth considering here. Firstly, ACV helps to balance the acidic levels within the stomach. Acid reflux is seen as an imbalance in the stomach, whereby acid spurts up from the stomach into the esophagus, thus creating heartburn. However, from a holistic point of view, acid reflux is not caused by unusual acid activity, but rather insufficient stomach acid levels cause it. Where ACV helps is that it balances the pH environment in the stomach, thus helping to normalize acidic stomach activity. So, even though ACV, like wheatgrass, acts as a base on the body, ACV is an acid, so while it converts into a base after digestion, before digestion it is acidic, and it helps the stomach balance its acid levels!

The second advantage is that it works while promoting an acidic environment in the stomach, which encourages lactobacilli, which are helpful bacteria that thrive in an acidic environment and help to maintain a healthy gut and kill off gut fungi such as candida!

ACV is very convenient to take; put one tablespoon of ACV in a glass and add in 250 ml (eight ounces) of water, stir with a spoon and drink. Be careful and understand that ACV is acidic, so make sure you wash your teeth by rinsing your mouth out with some water or another beverage afterward to wash away the acidic deposits from the teeth. Other than that, ACV is easy to take, although it is bitter. Also, the ideal ACV is slightly smoky because it possesses a string of material known as "the mother", which is very potent. So, when buying ACV, try to get the version that is a little bit misty.

ACV will have a general balancing effect on gut health and is helpful for people who suffer from acid reflux problems. However, it's not the sort of supplement you take when you have acute acid reflux symptoms. When you are suffering from acid reflux, and you want to treat the symptom, take an antacid, natural yogurt, or low-fat milk. But get into the habit of drinking at least one glass a day of ACV, and after some weeks, it will have an impact on stomach acid and gut health in general.

Also, ACV goes well with wheatgrass. I find that washing down a glass of ACV with a glass of wheatgrass is an excellent way to get my daily quota of both, and, of course, the wheatgrass washes off the acidic ACV deposits from my teeth as wheatgrass is a base.

Kombucha

Kombucha is a popular health drink; it is a sugary black tea, which, after fermentation, becomes laden with healthy bacteria, vinegar, B vitamins, probiotics, enzymes and healthy acids (acetic, lactic and gluconic).

Benefits of kombucha include:

- Gut health
- Weight loss
- Detoxification
- Improved immune system
- Reduced joint pain
- Anti-cancerous

In particular, in terms of gut health, the great thing about kombucha is its fantastic variety of probiotics, which help to keep the digestive process working correctly.

Kombucha is high in acetobacter, gluconacetobacte, lactobacillus and zygosaccharomyces probiotics. So it will go a long way towards getting your gut to work well. With so many probiotics, these will flush out funguses (such as candida) and aid digestion.

Also, kombucha is high in free antioxidants, which help to counteract free radicals in the gut and also aid digestive health. Kombucha has also been known to treat stomach ulcers and prevent and treat leaky gut syndrome.

Kombucha is a potent gut health tonic and one or two glasses a day will go a long way towards improving stomach and gut health. But do note that there are so many probiotics in kombucha that if your gut is out of balance, initially it might result in symptoms such as bloatedness, gas, mild stomach ache, and diarrhea. Don't worry about this as it is the gut's way of normalizing under the powerful and potent impact of kombucha. So, when you start taking kombucha, ease into it by drinking one glass a day for a few days, and then build up to two or three glasses a day. Then, after a few weeks when you feel things settle down, reduce back to a maintenance level of one glass a day.

Kefir: Kefir is a Turkish cultured dairy product, which is very high in probiotics. It has been used as a health food for centuries, and amongst its many benefits are:

- Improves immunity levels
- Heals gut problems
- Helps digest lactose
- Kills off candida fungus
- Treats allergies
- Strengthens bones
- Detoxicant

Kefir's many benefits come from its nutrient-rich make-up. It is high in vitamin B12, vitamin K2, calcium, biotin, folate, probiotics, and enzymes. In particular, enzymes and probiotics make kefir a very potent gut health food.

Enzymes reduce once one reaches 30 years of age, which, in turn, makes it more difficult to digest food, so eating a supplement that is high in digestive enzymes is a great way of improving digestion. Secondly, probiotics are healthy bacteria, and they help prevent nasty digestive fungi such as candida, for example.

Kefir is jam-packed with probiotics, which include bifidobacteria, acetobacter, lactobacillus acidophilus, lactobacillus bulgaricus, lactobacillus caucasus, lactobacillus rhamnosus, lactobacillus, and leuconostoc.

The result of this is that kefir can heal many gut issues including leaky gut syndrome. Also, interestingly, it helps people who suffer from lactose intolerance to start absorbing lactose!

For anyone who is suffering from gut health issues, kefir is worth trying out. However, kefir is a dairy product, so it might be challenging to take for anyone who is lactose intolerant. People who suffer from candida, for example, are lactose intolerant, so they won't initially be able to absorb kefir. Make an effort to detoxify and clean up your digestive system in the first place. So, take other supplements such as wheatgrass, ACV, and ginger for a while, and then slowly add in the kefir.

Moringa

Moringa is a tree that grows prolifically in Southeast Asia and is often referred to as the "miracle tree" because it is very high in nutrients including beta carotene, vitamin C, carotene and protein.

Moringa is so high in nutrients that it has 12 times more vitamin C than an orange, 10 times more vitamin A than carrots, and 17 times more calcium than milk, for example!

In terms of gut health, moringa can help in several ways. For a start, it is high in antioxidants, which help to detox the intestines. Secondly, moringa helps to reduce inflammation in the body. Inflammation is the body's way of coping with imbalances in the body; it's a sort of cordon whereby the body cordons off infected areas. For a short time, it works well, but after a while, chronic health develops. Inflammation in the gut is a bad thing as it makes food nutrient absorption difficult and also the excretion of waste difficult. So, moringa can help to reduce inflammation through the body, which includes the gut. Moreover, moringa boosts liver functioning, which helps to detoxify the system, which is good as where there is a dysfunctional gut, there will be a buildup of toxins in the body.

Moringa leaves can be used with your meals as in a salad or a juice, for example. If you can't get raw moringa, you can probably get a hold of organic cold-pressed moringa oil. Moringa oil is expensive, but it's potent with about a tablespoonful a day being a perfect overall health tonic and, of course, a gut treatment for gut health problems.

Supplements for Gut Health

So far, we have looked at foods that help to cure gut health problems, but there are also some supplements that can help. So, let's take a look.

Deglycyrrhizinated licorice (DGL)

Licorice is perfect for health and helps cure, or improve, a wide range of health conditions. However, long-term usage can harm blood pressure levels, edema, and estrogen levels, thanks to the presence of glycyrrhizin. Deglycyrrhizinated licorice has all the benefits of licorice but without the potential downsides of glycyrrhizin.

In regards to gut health, DGL provides excellent relief for heartburn, peptic ulcers, and gastritis, which relates to its anti-inflammatory properties and its gut bacteria-balancing properties. In a study of 82 patients who took DGL, versus an over-the-counter peptic ulcer medication, the patients who were given two DGL tablets daily over a period of two years demonstrated the same level of reoccurrence of peptic ulcers as the patients who took the peptic ulcer medicine, which suggests that DGL is as strong as the allopathic medication!

They also note noted in this study that the DGL group, just like the pharmaceutical group, suffered from a significant increase in the onset of peptic ulcers after they stopped taking DGL. This suggests that while DGL is as effective as pharmaceutical medications at treating peptic ulcers, it only keeps peptic ulcers at bay as long as it is taken. So, for some people who suffer extreme stomach issues, such as peptic ulcers, DGL will probably end up becoming part of a lifelong treatment plan!

Regarding dosage, usually, DGL is taken anywhere from one to three tablets, at a dosage of 380 to 400 mg per tablet. Taking the DGL tablet about 30 minutes before each meal will help relieve your stomach.

With that in mind, it's important to remember that long-term herbal supplement use can have toxic side effects, just like long-term medications can. With DGL, the majority of the glycyrrhizin has been removed. However, a little remains, so if you decide to use DGL over a long period, do check your blood pressure,from time to time and watch out for edema. Also, in some cases, liver toxicity can occur. Deglycyrrhizinated licorice is a great supplement and chances are there will be no side effects, but this is something to bear in mind for anyone who is on long-term medication, and DGL being just as effective as a pharmaceutical drug should be respected as potentially damaging to health, in some cases.

As to why you should use DGL rather than using pharmaceutical drugs, DGL, being a natural product, will have fewer side effects, but, like any powerful herb, some toxic side effects shall remain present.

And this is something to remember with the various foods,

supplements, and health tips mentioned in this book. In an ideal world, every health condition would be curable, but in reality, gut health can vary from individual to individual. Some people will get significant relief from their symptoms with a few small changes. Anyone who suffers from a strong food allergy can testify to this! However, for some people, no matter how many strategies they try, or foods they take, their gut health issues linger on. For people in this group, the thing to remember is that gut health is a complex topic and although a full-blown cure may not come, certainly with patience and application of good healing strategies, foods, and supplements, much relief can be achieved.

So, if you have tried everything under the sun and yet still suffer from gut health issues, then don't despair. Things will get better, but some trial and error may be required, and even if a full recovery does not come, certainly a great improvement can be made. The reason for writing this book is to share some resources with you that you might not have already considered. While modern health care can help in many ways, there is a tendency to treat patients symptomatically by providing different drugs to treat various symptoms. I'm not saying that complementary health care is better but that it provides us with some more resources and other options. Also, it focuses upon balance, and where a rebalance can take place often symptoms will take care of themselves!

Betaine Hydrochloric Acid

Betaine Hydrochloric Acid is an ideal supplement for people who are suffering from insufficient stomach acid levels. As noted earlier, from a complementary point of view, acid reflux is a direct consequence of deficient stomach acid levels, which result in sporadic production of hydrochloric acid in the stomach, some of which ends up in the esophagus, which results in acid reflux symptoms. Apple cider vinegar can help to restore this balance as ACV is an acid, but for more severe cases, if ACV doesn't appear to help, it's worth trying betaine hydrochloric acid.

Betaine HCL will help to rebalance the acid levels in the stomach, which will not only cure acid reflux but also it helps to improve the overall health and vitality of the stomach and gut, and, finally, sufficient levels of HCL are required to effectively break down and digest vitamin B12, amino acids, and proteins!

Regarding dosage, a little bit of trial and error is required. Start by taking a meal that contains at least 20 grams of protein (HCL is required to break down the protein). Take one betaine HCL pill (around 650 mg) and check in with your stomach, after eating, to check whether there is any difference to digestion. You should feel better, but if you feel a burning sensation, the chances are that too much acid has been taken. If you feel a burning distension feeling, then reduce down to half a pill. Whether you feel an improvement or don't feel any improvement, maintain this one pill per meal and after a couple of days try out two pills and see how you feel. Keep experimenting with the dosage until you feel an improvement in digestion but don't feel any discomfort. Once you feel discomfort, stop, and even reduce the dosage a little bit if need be.

So, experiment a little bit until you are taking enough betaine HCL to make an excellent improvement to digestion without overdoing it as too much HCL will make you feel ill. For most people, the dose of betaine HCL shall be somewhere between 3000 mg and 5500 mg per meal. Taking too little won't do anything to help digestion but make the gut environment overly acidic.

Contraindications

One thing you have to be careful about when using betaine HCL is when it is mixed with anti-inflammatory drugs such as aspirin, corticosteroids, indocin, ibuprofen, and NSAIDs (a non-steroidal anti-inflammatory drug) in general. The reason is that HCL pills, when mixed into a stomach that already contains these drugs, can aggravate the stomach lining and even result in bleeding of the stomach lining or even the development of an ulcer!

So, while betaine HCL is a great way to improve acid reflux and indigestion, you have to be careful; otherwise, you can make things worse!

Also, anti-inflammatory drugs are very popular; ibuprofen, for example (Motrin, Advil, and Brofen), is a top-rated headache pill, and, of course, aspirin is very popular, so check out your medications and don't mix these medications with HCL!

L-Glutamine

L-Glutamine is a beneficial supplement. It is an amino acid, being the most common amino acid used by the human body (around 30 present of all amino acid nitrogen in the blood is L-glutamine). Being an amino acid, L-Glutamine will be a big help in building muscle and maintaining lean muscle when dieting, but it also comes with many other benefits, which include:

- It is excellent for intestinal health as it helps to rebuild and repair damage to the gut
- It helps to heal ulcers, cure leaky gut syndrome and prevent further damage to the stomach and intestines
- It improves symptoms of irritable bowel syndrome (IBS) and diarrhea by balancing mucus levels in the stomach lining
- Reduces cravings for sweets and alcohol
- Improves metabolism
- Detoxifies the body (including the intestines)
- Improves blood sugar control
- Anti-cancer agent
- Promotes muscle growth and prevents muscle wasting
- Improves athletic performance and recovery from exercise

So, in essence, L-glutamine is a bodybuilder that helps to repair gut health issues.

In a study of 20 patients who were fed intravenously for two weeks, they noted that the group who received L-glutamine along with the intravenous food suffered less gastrointestinal degeneration and demonstrated better permeability than those who didn't. Intravenous feeding harms digestive health, so this study shows the potency of L-glutamine.

In another study, they noted the healing mechanism of L-glutamine, whereby it regulates the IgA immune response. IgA is an antibody that fights against harmful bacteria and viruses. It also relates to food sensitivities and allergies. So, taking L-glutamine will help with food intolerances.

In yet another study in the *Journal of Clinical Immunology*, they discovered that L-glutamine regulates the TH2 immune response, which, in turn, regulates inflammatory cytokines. What this means is that L-glutamine reduces inflammatory responses, which, in turn, helps to reduce many gut imbalances.

In summary, L-glutamine can repair damage, reduce food sensitivity and allergic responses, and also reduce or even eliminate the inflammatory effect.

L-glutamine is a must-have supplement for anyone who is facing gut repair issues. Leaky gut syndrome, for example, isn't just uncomfortable, it also promotes other degenerative health conditions, such as autoimmune conditions, psoriasis, arthritis, and even Hashimoto's disease (a slow thyroid).

When we think about healing gut issues, we have to think in terms of getting rid of toxins, righting imbalances, and also repairing organic damage, and this is where L-glutamine comes in handy.

L-glutamine helps with repairing damage caused by a wide variety of gut health issues including Crohn's disease, irritable bowel syndrome (IBS), ulcerative colitis, diverticulosis, and diverticulitis, for example.

How to Take L-Glutamine

L-glutamine comes in two forms, the first of which is free form, which has to be taken with food for proper absorption. The other type is known as trans-alanyl glutamine or alanyl –L - glutamine. The latter is more absorbable than free form L-glutamine, so you can take it on an empty stomach if you want to. You can take it after your meals, and, in particular, it is helpful either before or after workouts in the gym as it supports both athletic performance and repair of muscle damage.

Regarding dosage, it is usually two to five grams a day, but up to 10 grams a day can be taken. For people with gut health, it makes the most sense to take it three times a day, during mealtime either before or after food to help with the digestive process. Also, for long-term use, it is a good idea to supplement some vitamin B12 every day, which helps to regulate L-glutamine levels in the body as L-glutamine can result in some toxicity if too much builds up in the body.

Side effects of too much L-glutamine include increased sweating in feet and hands, back pain, joint pain, muscle pain, dizziness, fatigue, headache, runny nose, dry mouth, gas, vomiting and stomach pain. These are unlikely to happen, but it's good to know. The vitamin B12 should minimize the tendency of side effects, but if some of these symptoms arise, then reduce the dosage accordingly.

Contraindications: L-glutamine should be avoided for people who are suffering from liver or kidney dysfunction.

Aloe Vera

Aloe vera is a super plant that has many great benefits, which include:

- High in anti-inflammatory properties

- Helps relieve constipation
- Promotes regular bowel movements
- Detoxification
- Encourages good gut bacteria
- Helps treat leaky gut syndrome
- Helps relieve heartburn/acid reflux
- High in antioxidants and antibacterial properties
- Fights off candida fungus
- Fights off parasitic infections
- Treats mouth ulcers
- Reduces dental plaque
- Improves skin quality
- Prevents wrinkles

In summary, aloe vera is a fantastic plant that demonstrates a wide range of effects. In particular, it works wonderfully well on gut health.

Aloe vera is high in nutrients, including calcium, copper, chromium, magnesium, manganese, potassium, sodium, selenium, and zinc. It is high in antioxidant vitamins A, C, and E; it is also a great source of vitamin B12, choline, and folic acid. Furthermore, it contains eight digestive enzymes (alianase, amylase, alkaline phosphatase, catalase, carboxypeptidase, cellulose, lipase, and peroxidase), which help to break down foods. Also, aloe vera is high in probiotics (healthy gut bacteria), which help to restore the balance of gut health. In a study on the effect of aloe vera on lactobacilli probiotics, they noted a significant increase in levels of L. acidophilus, L. Plantarum and L. casei, via aloe vera supplementation. Finally, aloe vera promotes regulation of pH levels throughout the body, which, in turn, aids gut health.

How to Take Aloe Vera

There is a variety of ways in which you can take aloe vera. You can take it as a juice or as a capsule. Regarding dosage, you can start with a small amount, say one teaspoon twice a day taken before meals. Slowly increase the dosage up to a maximum of four tablespoons twice a day. How much you will take depends on your gut health issues and your reaction to aloe vera juice or capsules. Aloe vera promotes bowel movements, so it is a good idea to take a small amount, particularly at first, since it will help to clear any backlog within the intestines, hence too much too soon might result in diarrhea-like symptoms!

Also, on the other hand, many people avoid aloe vera, believing it to be a laxative, but it is quite safe to take, and even kids can take it, but they should take a minimal amount like a teaspoon or two per day. Aloe vera is safe, but it does rebalance bowel movements and can result in a laxative effect if you take too much too soon!

Chapter 12: Recipes

BREAKFAST

Quinoa Porridge

Prep time: 5 minutes

Servings: 4

Ingredients:

- Quinoa, ¾ c.
- Low-fat almond milk, 1½ c.
- Splenda, 3 tbsps.
- Vanilla extract, ½ tsp.
- Salt.

Directions:

1. Boil milk in a cooking pot and whisk in quinoa.
2. Stir, cook the mixture until smooth and creamy.
3. Add salt, vanilla, and Splenda.
4. Serve.

Nutritional Info: Calories: 544, Fat: 24.9 g, Carbs: 30.7 g, Protein: 6.4 g

Banana Bread

Prep time: 10 minutes

Servings: 4

Ingredients:

- Vanilla extract, 1 tsp.
- Salt.
- Splenda, ¾ c.
- Coconut Flour, 1 ½ c.
- Baking soda, 1 tsp.
- Melted almond butter, 1/3 c.
- Peeled bananas, 3.

Directions:

1. Adjust your oven to 350 degrees F to preheat.

2. Grease a 4x8 inch bread pan with almond butter.

3. Mash bananas in a glass bowl and whisk in melted almond butter.

4. Mix baking soda with salt in another bowl.

5. Add Splenda, vanilla extract, and whisked egg.

6. Stir in flour and mix well until smooth.

7. Transfer the batter into the greased pan.

8. Bake for 50 minutes.

9. Slice and serve.

Nutritional Info: Calories: 387, Fat: 6 g, Protein: 6.6 g, Carbs: 37.4 g

Apricot Oats

Prep time: 15 minutes

Servings: 4

Ingredients:

- Egg whites, 5.
- Chopped soft dried figs, 1/3 c.
- Ground ginger, 1 tsp.
- Chopped soft pitted dates, ¼ c.
- Whole rolled oats, 2 c.
- Chopped soft dried apricots, ½ c.
- Dried coconut, 1/6 c.

Directions:

1. Set the oven to 150 degrees C.

2. Layer a baking sheet with parchment paper.

3. Mix everything in a bowl except egg whites.

4. Stir in egg whites and mix again.

5. Spread the mixture in the baking tray.

6. Bake for 40 mins approximately.

7. Slice and serve.

Nutritional Info: Calories: 519, Fat: 31.4 g, Protein: 6.5 g, Carbs: 57.8 g

Vegetable Tacos

Prep time: 15 minutes

Servings: 2
Ingredients:

- Olive oil, 1 tbsp.
- Mashed canned black beans, 1 c.
- Corn tortillas, 12.
- Ground cumin, 1 tsp.
- Lime zest, ½.
- Ground coriander, ½ tsp.
- Small diced sweet potato, 1.
- Medium sliced and peeled carrot, 1.
- Kosher salt, ¼ tsp.

Directions:
1. Preheat the oven to 350 degrees F. Line small cookie sheet with baking paper.

2. Mix carrots and sweet potatoes with oil, lime zest, salt, coriander and cumin in a small-sized bowl. Transfer the mixture to cookie sheet. Roast at 350F for 12–15 minutes.

3. After vegetables are done, spread mashed beans on tortillas. Top with vegetables. Serve.

Nutritional Info: Calories: 297, Protein: 10 g, Carbs: 48 g, Fat: 8 g

Ginger and Banana Smoothies

Prep time: 10 minutes

Servings: 2

Ingredients:

- Pure honey, 1 tbsp.
- Small ripe bananas, 2.
- Unsweetened fat-free yogurt, 1 c.
- Ice, 1 c.
- Low-fat milk, 1½ c.
- Peeled grated ginger, ½ tsp.

Directions:

1. Peel bananas. Chop into the food processor.

2. Add the ginger, milk, ice, and yogurt and blend till the consistency is smooth.
Add honey. Blend for several seconds.

3. Serve.

Nutritional Info: Calories: 333, Protein: 14 g, Carbs: 69 g, Fat: 2 g

Banana and Mango Smoothie

Prep time: 10 minutes

Servings: 1

Ingredients:

- Natural, fat-free yogurt, 2 c.
- Peeled and chopped banana, 1.
- Segmented pink small fruit, 1.
- Ice cubes.
- Halved, stoned and chopped mango, 1.

Directions:

1. Blend mango, pink fruit, and banana in a blender, along with yogurt and ice cubes.

2. Serve.

Nutritional Info: Calories: 134, Fat: 4.7 g, Carbs: 54.1 g, Protein: 6.2 g

Sweet Potato Tarts

Prep time: 40 minutes

Servings: 12

Ingredients:

- Large eggs, 2.
- Sweet potatoes, 20 oz.
- Low-fat milk, ¾ c.
- Granulated Splenda, 2 tbsps.
- Pure vanilla extract, 2 tsp.
- Kosher salt, 1/8 tsp.
- Ginger snap cookies, 4 oz.
- Filtered water quarts, 4.
- Maple syrup, 1 tbsp.

Directions:

1. Preheat oven to 325F.
2. Place water in a large-sized pot on high heat.
3. Add sweet potatoes. When the water boils, reduce the heat and simmer.
4. Cook sweet potatoes for 35–40 minutes, till you can easily slip a knife into the middle.
5. Remove sweet potatoes to plate lined with paper towels. Let them cool.
6. Place ginger snaps in a food processor with a steel blade. Process till crumbs are medium-sized.
7. Pulse processor while you drizzle in maple syrup.
8. Line standard muffin tin with foil papers.
9. Evenly distribute ginger snap cookie mixture in foil inside muffin cups. Pat gently down.
10. Place muffin pan in the oven. Cook for 8–10 minutes and remove the pan from oven.

11. Mash sweet potatoes till smooth. Then whisk in egg yolks, salt, vanilla, Splenda, and milk.
12. Whisk egg whites in a separate bowl till they have formed stiff peaks.

13. Fold egg whites gently into sweet potato mixture. Then scoop batter into muffin cups. Bake for 35–40 minutes. Allow it to cool. Chill and serve.

Nutritional Info: Calories: 119, Protein: 2 g, Carbs: 22 g, Fat: 2 g

Sweet Potato Toast with Almond Butter

Prep time: 20 minutes

Servings: 2

Ingredients:

- Ground ginger, ¼ tsp.
- Almond butter, 3 tbsps.
- Organic honey, ½ tsp.
- Peeled medium sweet potato, 1.
- Peeled medium kiwis, 2.

Directions:

1. Slice the sweet potato in ¼ " lengthways slices.
2. Stir honey, almond butter, and ginger together in a small-sized bowl till combined well.

3. Toast sliced sweet potatoes on the high setting of toaster till they become soft and thoroughly cooked. It could take two or more rounds of toasting to achieve that.

4. Spread one side of all slices with honey mixture. Top with the sliced kiwis. Serve.

Nutritional Info: Calories: 277, Protein: 8 g, Carbs: 35 g, Fat: 14 g

Chicken with Fennel Turmeric

Prep time: 35 minutes

Servings: 4

Ingredients:

- Skinless and de-boned chicken breasts, 4.
- Ground turmeric, 1 tsp.
- Ground fennel seed, ½ tsp.
- Kosher salt, ¼ tsp.
- Olive oil, 2 tsp.

Directions:

1. Preheat the oven to 375F. Line cookie sheet with baking paper.
2. Mix oil, salt, turmeric, and fennel in a small-sized bowl.
3. Place chicken breasts on the cookie sheet. Brush with oil mixture.

4. Transfer to oven. Bake the chicken for 20–25 minutes. Internal temperature should read 160F. Allow to cool a bit, then slice and serve.

Nutritional Info: Calories: 158, Protein: 26 g, Carbs: 0 g, Fat: 5 g

English Muffins

Prep time: 10 minutes

Servings: 4

Ingredients:

- Coconut Flour, 4 ½ c.
- Salt, 1 ½ tsp.
- Lightly beaten egg white, 1.
- Splenda, 2 tbsps.
- Semolina, 2 tbsps.
- Low fat almond milk, 1 ¾ c.
- Instant yeast, 2 tsp.
- Softened almond butter, 3.

Directions:

1. Mix all the muffin ingredients in a mixing bowl, except semolina.
2. Blend the ingredients using an electric mixer to form a smooth dough.
3. Let the dough rest for 2 hours.
4. Grease 2 muffin trays with cooking oil and sprinkle semolina into each cup.
5. Knead the raised dough and divide it into 16 equal pieces.
6. Roll each piece into small balls.
7. Place the balls in the muffin trays and cover them.
8. Allow them to rest for 20 minutes.
9. Bake for 15 mins on low heat in the preheated oven until golden.
10. Serve.

Nutritional Info: Calories: 212, Fat: 11.8 g, Carbs: 14.6 g, Protein: 17.3 g

Poached Eggs Spinach

Prep time: 10 minutes

Servings: 2

Ingredients:

- Baby spinach, 1 bunch.
- Large eggs, 4.
- Kosher salt, ¼ tsp.

Directions:

1. In 12" skillet, add one inch of water.
2. Add one tsp. of salt. Bring to simmer on med. Then heat.
3. Crack eggs into four custard dishes or ramekins.
4. Pour eggs carefully into the water at simmer one after another.
5. Turn heat off. Cover pan, and allow to set for five minutes.
6. After five minutes, remove eggs carefully with a slotted spoon.
7. Serve poached eggs promptly atop baby spinach bed. Serve.

Nutritional Info: Calories: 149, Protein: 9 g, Carbs: 21 g, Fat: 5 g

Muesli-Style Oatmeal

Prep time: 5 minutes

Servings: 1

Ingredients:

- Peeled and diced apple.
- Raisins, 2 tbsps.
- Splenda, 2 tsp.
- Low fat almond milk, 1 c.
- Oatmeal, 1 c.
- Salt, ¼ tsp.

Directions:

1. Soak oatmeal in milk along with salt, Splenda, and raisins in a glass bowl.
2. Cover and refrigerate the bowl for 2 hours.
3. Stir in apples.
4. Serve.

Nutritional Info: Calories: 519, Fat: 31.4 g, Carbs: 57.8 g, Protein: 6.5 g

Banana-Flax Smoothie

Prep Time: 5 Minutes

Servings: 2

Ingredients:

- 1 banana
- 1½ c.low-fat nondairy milk (like rice milk)
- 2 tbsps. flaxseed
- ¼ tsp. vanilla extract
- One packet stevia
- ½ c. crushed ice

Directions:

In a blender, combine all the ingredients and blend until smooth. Serve.

Nutritional Info: Calories: 138, Protein: 3 g, Fat: 7 g, Carbs: 18 g

Sweet Melon Smoothie

Prep Time: 5 Minutes

Servings: 2

Ingredients:

- 1½ c. chopped cantaloupe or other melon
- 1½ c.low-fat nondairy milk (rice milk)
- ½ c. lactose-free plain nonfat yogurt
- ¼ tsp. fennel seed
- ½ c. crushed ice

Directions:

In a blender, combine all the ingredients and blend until smooth. Serve.

Nutritional Info: Calories: 108, Protein: 5 g, Fat: 3 g, Carbs: 16 g

Green Aloe Vera Smoothie

Prep Time: 5 Minutes

Servings: 2

Ingredients:

- 1½ c. baby spinach
- ¼ c. parsley, fresh
- ½ banana
- 1½ c. aloe vera
- ½ c. ice, crushed

Directions:

In a blender, combine all the ingredients and blend until smooth. Serve.

Nutritional Info: Calories: 158, Protein: 3 g, Fat: <1 g, Carbs: 39 g

Chia Breakfast Pudding with Cantaloupe

Prep time: 5 minutes

Servings: 4

Ingredients:

- 2 c. low-fat rice milk
- ¼ c. honey
- ½ tsp. vanilla extract
- ½ c. chia seeds
- 1 c. chopped cantaloupe

Directions:

1. In a bowl, whisk together the milk, honey, and vanilla.
2. Stir in the chia seeds. Cover and refrigerate overnight (or for at least 4 hours).
3. Serve the cantaloupe spooned over the pudding.

Nutritional Info: Calories: 206, Protein: 7 g, Fat: 7 g, Carbs: 34 g

Fruit and Yogurt Parfait

Prep time: 10 minutes

Servings: 2

Ingredients:

- 2 c. lactose-free plain nonfat yogurt
- 3 tbsps. pure maple syrup
- ¼ tsp. ginger, ground
- ½ banana, peeled and sliced
- ¼ c. pecans, chopped

Directions:

1. In a small bowl, whisk together the yogurt, syrup, and ginger.
2. Spoon ½ cup of the yogurt mixture into each of the two parfait glasses.
3. Top each with half of the banana slices.
4. Top each with another ½ cup yogurt mixture.
5. Sprinkle each with two tablespoons pecans. Serve.

Nutritional Info: Calories: 354, Protein: 14 g, Fat: 14 g, Carbs: 46 g

Maple-Ginger Oatmeal

Prep time: 5 minutes

Servings: 2

Ingredients:

- 1½ c. water
- Pinch salt
- 1 c. old-fashioned rolled oats
- ¼ c. pure maple syrup
- ½ tsp. ground ginger

Directions:

1. In a small pot, bring the water and salt to a boil over medium-high heat.
2. Stir in the oats, syrup, and ginger.
3. Reduce the heat to medium-low. Cook, frequently stirring for 5 minutes. Serve.

Nutritional Info: Calories: 258, Protein: 7 g, Fat: 3 g, Carbs: 53 g

Corn Porridge with Maple and Raisins

Prep time: 5 minutes

Servings: 2

Ingredients:

- ¾ c. cornmeal
- 2¼ c. water, divided
- Pinch salt
- 1 tbsp. pure maple syrup
- 3 tbsps. raisins

Directions:

1. In a small bowl, whisk together the cornmeal and ¾ cup of water.
2. In a small pot, bring the remaining 1½ cups of water and the salt to a boil over medium-high heat.
3. Whisk in the cornmeal slurry. Cook, stirring, for 10 to 12 minutes, until thick.
4. Stir in the maple syrup, and raisins. Then serve hot.

Nutritional Info: Calories: 288, Protein: 6 g, Fat: 3 g, Carbs: 60 g

Milky Oat

Prep time: 8 minutes

Servings: 2

Ingredients:

- 1 c. oats
- ½ c. low-fat coconut milk
- ½ c. water
- 1 tsp. liquid stevia

Directions:

1. Mix up together the coconut milk and water in the saucepan.
2. Add oats and stir.
3. Close the lid and cook the oats over the medium heat for 10 minutes.
4. When the oats are cooked, let them chill for 5–10 minutes.
5. Then add liquid stevia and stir it.
6. After this, transfer the milky oat to the bowls and serve!

Nutritional Info: Calories: 293, Fat: 17 g, Carbs: 31 g, Protein: 6.8 g

Coconut Quinoa

Prep time: 10 minutes

Servings: 6

Ingredients:

- 2 c. quinoa
- 1 c.low-fat coconut milk
- 1 c. water
- 2 tbsps. coconut syrup

Directions:

1. Pour coconut milk and water into the saucepan.
2. Add quinoa and stir it.
3. After this, close the lid and cook the quinoa for 15 minutes or until it is cooked.
4. Transfer the cooked quinoa into the serving bowls and sprinkle with the coconut syrup. Serve it!

Nutritional Info: Calories: 312, Fat: 13 g, Carbs: 41.3 g, Protein: 8.9 g

Chia Quinoa

Prep time: 10 minutes

Servings: 4

Ingredients:

- 1 c.low-fat coconut milk
- 1 c. quinoa
- 1 c. water
- 4 tsps. chia seeds
- 1 tbsp. coconut syrup
- 1 tsp. shredded coconut
- ½ tsp. vanilla extract

Directions:

1. Pour the coconut milk into the saucepan.
2. Add quinoa and close the lid.
3. Cook the quinoa for 15 minutes.
4. Meanwhile, mix up together the almond milk, water, and chia seeds.
5. When the quinoa is cooked, chill it thoroughly.
6. Add vanilla extract and coconut syrup.
7. Stir it and add chia seeds.
8. Then stir the breakfast and transfer in the serving bowls.
9. Decorate the quinoa bowls with the shredded coconut and serve!

Nutritional Info: Calories: 375, Fat: 21.4 g, Carbs: 38.7 g, Protein: 9.7 g

Breakfast Muesli

Prep time: 10 minutes

Servings:4

Ingredients:

- 1 tbsp. almond meal
- 2 tbsps. oats
- 1 tbsp. flax seeds
- 2 tbsps. chopped almonds
- ½ tsp. chia seeds
- 1 tbsp. pumpkin seeds
- 2 c. low-fat nut milk

Directions:

1. Mix up together the almond meal, oats, flax seeds, chopped almonds, and chia seeds in the big bowl.
2. Preheat the nut milk a little.
3. Add pumpkin seeds and nut milk.
4. Stir it gently and transfer to the serving bowls.
5. Enjoy!

Nutritional Info: Calories: 342, Fat: 33.2 g, Carbs: 11 g, Protein: 5.2 g

Fast Porridge

Prep time: 10 minutes

Servings: 2

Ingredients:

- ¼ c. almonds, chopped
- 3 tbsps. chia seeds
- ¼ c. sunflower seeds
- 2 c.low-fat coconut milk
- 1 tbsp. barley grass powder

Directions:

1. Place the almonds, chia seeds, sunflower seeds, and barley grass powder in the serving bowls.
2. Stir the ingredients and add coconut milk.
3. Stir the porridge well and enjoy!

Nutritional Info: Calories: 793, Fat: 74.8 g, Carbs: 29.1 g, Protein: 13.9 g

Chia Breakfast

Prep time: 15 minutes

Servings: 4

Ingredients:

- 1 ½ c. quinoa
- 2 ½ c. water
- 8 tbsps. chia seeds
- 2 c.low-fat hemp milk
- 1 date, pitted
- 1 tbsp. almonds, chopped
- 1 tbsp. shredded coconut

Directions:

1. Pour water into the pan and add quinoa.
2. Close the lid and cook for 15 minutes.
3. When the quinoa is cooked, chill it little.
4. After this, place the hemp milk and pitted date in the blender.
5. Blend the mixture until smooth and transfer in the big bowl.
6. Add chia seeds and stir well.
7. After this, leave the mixture for 10 minutes more.
8. Then add cooked quinoa. Stir it.
9. Transfer the cooked breakfast to the serving bowls.
10. Sprinkle the meal with the chopped almonds and shredded coconut.
11. Enjoy!

Nutritional Info: Calories: 453, Fat: 17.3 g, Carbs: 60 g, Protein: 16.7 g

Apple Parfait

Prep time: 10 minutes

Servings: 2

Ingredients:

- 2 oz. cashews, soaked
- 2 oz.low-fat coconut milk
- ¼ tsp. vanilla extract
- 2 apples, chopped
- 1 tbsp. hemp seeds

Directions:

1. Place the cashews, coconut milk, vanilla extract, and hemp seeds into the blender.
2. Blend the mixture until smooth and homogenous.
3. After this, place the small amount of the smooth mixture in the glass.
4. Then make a layer of the chopped apples.
5. Repeat the layers until you have put in all the ingredients.
6. Serve it!

Nutritional Info: Calories: 367, Fat: 22 g, Carbs: 42 g, Protein: 6.8 g

Layered Oats

Prep time: 5 hours

Servings: 3

Ingredients:

- 1 c. oats
- 1 c. almond yogurt
- 1 c.figs, chopped
- ½ tsp. vanilla extract

Directions:

1. Mix up together the almond yogurt and oats in the big bowl.
2. Add vanilla extract and stir it.
3. After this, put the oat mixture in the glass jars in a small layer.
4. After this, make a layer of the chopped figs.
5. Then add a layer of the oats.
6. Put the oat mixture on the top of the glass jars as the last layer and place in the fridge for 5 hours. Enjoy!

Nutritional Info: Calories: 197, Fat: 7.3 g, Carbs: 28.6 g, Protein: 5.3 g

Chia Seed Pudding

Prep time: 5 hours

Servings: 2

Ingredients:

- 3 oz. chia seeds
- 1 oz. almonds, soaked
- 1 c.low-fat hemp milk
- 2 oz.figs
- 1 tsp. liquid stevia

Directions:

1. Chop the almonds and put them in 2 mason jars.
2. Then add chia seeds, liquid stevia, and figs.
3. After this, add hemp milk and stir the mixture well.
4. Seal the lids and place the meal in the fridge.
5. Leave the chia pudding in the fridge for at least 5 hours.
6. Enjoy!

Nutritional Info: Calories: 360, Fat: 23.8 g, Carbs: 28.6 g, Protein: 12.8 g

Scrambled Eggs

Prep time: 8 minutes

Servings: 4

Ingredients:

- 4 eggs, whisked
- 2 oz. watercress
- 4 slices of gluten-free rye bread
- 3 tsps. low fat almond milk
- 1 tsp.olive oil
- 1 pinch of salt

Directions:

1. Mix up together the whisked eggs and almond milk. Add salt and stir it gently.
2. Place the olive oil in the frying pan and preheat it.
3. After this, add the whisked egg mixture and cook it for 1 minute over the medium-high heat.
4. After this, stir the eggs well (scramble them) and cook for 30 seconds more.
5. Scramble the eggs one more time and cook with the closed lid for 2 minutes more over the low heat.
6. Aftrer cooking the scrambled eggs, transfer them over the rye bread slices and add the watercress.
7. Serve!

Nutritional Info: Calories 102, Fat: 6.7 g, Carbs: 4 g, Protein: 6.6 g

Watermelon Salad

Prep time: 10 minutes

Servings: 5

Ingredients:

- 15 oz. watermelon, seeded, chopped
- 1 c. spinach, chopped
- 1 tsp. flax seeds
- 1 tsp. low-fat almond milk

Directions:

1. Combine the watermelon, spinach, and flax seeds in the salad bowl.
2. Stir it.
3. Make the dressing by stirring the almond milk.
4. Sprinkle the watermelon salad with the almond milk dressing and serve without stirring.
5. Enjoy!

Nutritional Info: Calories: 34, Fat: 0.5 g, Carbs: 7.5 g, Protein: 0.8 g

Delicious Avocado Smoothie

Prep time: 10 minutes

Servings: 4

Ingredients:

- 10 oz. cucumber, chopped
- 5 c. spinach, chopped
- 12 oz. broccoli, chopped
- 2 avocados, peeled, pitted
- 1 c. ice
- 1 tbsp. stevia extract
- 1 c.low-fat almond milk

Directions:

1. Put the chopped cucumbers and spinach in the blender and blend for 10 seconds.
2. After this, add broccoli and avocado.
3. Blend the mixture for 30 seconds more.
4. Then chop the lemon and add it to the mixture.
5. Add ice and stevia extract.
6. After this, add almond milk and blend the mixture for 3 minutes at the maximum speed.
7. After cooking the smoothie, pour it into the glasses and serve!

Nutritional Info: Calories: 395, Fat: 34.5 g, Carbs: 22.9 g, Protein: 7.4 g

Breakfast Shake

Prep time: 10 minutes

Servings: 4

Ingredients:

- ½ c. almonds, soaked, peeled
- 2 avocados, peeled, pitted
- 1 c. kale, chopped
- ¼ tsp. fresh ginger, peeled
- 1 c. coconut water
- ½ tsp.low-fat almond milk
- 1 tbsp. liquid stevia

Directions:

1. Place the almonds in the blender and blend well until smooth.
2. Then chop the avocados into the chunks and add the blended almond mixture.
3. After this, add kale and fresh ginger.
4. Then add almond milk and coconut water.
5. Pour the liquid stevia and blend the mixture at the maximum speed for 4 minutes or until homogenous and smooth.
6. Serve the cooked shake immediately!

Nutritional Info: Calories: 295, Fat: 25.8 g, Carbs: 15.3 g, Protein: 5.4 g

Banana Shake

Prep time: 10 minutes

Servings: 3

Ingredients:

- 4 bananas, frozen, chopped
- 1 c.low-fat almond milk
- 1 mango, chopped
- 1 tbsp. liquid stevia

Directions:

1. Put the frozen bananas and mango in the blender.
2. Blend the fruits at the maximum speed for 3 minutes.
3. After this, add liquid stevia and almond milk.
4. Blend the mixture well until smooth and liquid.
5. Pour the cooked shake into the glasses and serve!

Nutritional Info: Calories: 391, Fat: 20 g, Carbs: 57.1 g, Protein: 4.5 g

SNACKS, APPETIZERS, AND SIDES

Calm Carrot Salad

Prep time: 10 minutes

Servings: 2

Ingredients:

- Splenda, 2 tbsps.
- Raisins, 2 tbsps.
- Olive oil, 2 tsps.
- Salt, ¼ tsp.
- Mesclun greens, ¼ lb.
- Trimmed and grated carrots, 1 lb.
- Dried oregano, 1 tsp.

Directions:

1. Mix oregano, Splenda, salt, raisins, and olive oil in a medium bowl.

2. Toss in carrots and mix well to coat.

3. Adjust seasoning with salt.

4. Serve over mesclun greens.

Nutritional Info: Calories: 144, Fat: 0.4 g, Carbs: 8 g, Protein: 5.6 g

Millet Cauliflower Mash

Prep time: 10 minutes

Servings: 4

Ingredients:

- Tamari, 1 tsp.
- Water, 3 c.
- Cauliflower florets, 1 c.
- Parsley sprig.
- Millet, 1 c.
- Salt, ¼ tsp.

Directions:

1. Roast the millet in a nonstick pan for 5 minutes.

2. Boil water in a large pan on high heat then add cauliflower, salt, and millet.

3. Cover the dish with the lid then cook for 25 minutes on low heat.

4. Stir in tamari and cook for 5 minutes.

5. Lightly mash the cauliflower mixture.

6. Garnish with parsley and serve.

Nutritional Info: Calories: 454, Fat: 4 g, Carbs: 30 g, Protein: 4 g

Spinach and Dill Dip

Prep time: 5 minutes

Servings: 4

Ingredients:

- 2 c. baby spinach
- ½ tsp. grated lemon zest
- ¼ tsp. sea salt
- 1 c. lactose-free nonfat plain yogurt
- 2 tbsps. chopped fresh dill

Directions:

1. In a large nonstick skillet, add the spinach, lemon zest, and sea salt. Cook, stirring, until the spinach wilts, 2 to 3 minutes. Remove from the heat and allow the spinach to cool.

2. In a small bowl, combine the cooled spinach, yogurt, and dill, stirring to combine.

3. Serve.

Nutritional Info: Calories: 68, Protein: 4 g, Fat: 4 g, Carbs: 5 g

Zucchini Hummus

Prep time: 5 minutes

Servings: 4

Ingredients:

- 1 medium zucchini, chopped
- 1 tbsp. olive oil
- 1 tbsp. tahini
- 1 tsp. chopped fresh dill
- ½ tsp. grated lemon zest
- ½ tsp. sea salt

Directions:

In a blender or food processor, combine all the ingredients. Blend until smooth. Serve.

Nutritional Info: Calories: 53, Protein: 1g, Fat: 5g, Carbs: 1g

Zucchini and Salmon Canapés

Prep time: 15 minutes

Servings: 4

Ingredients:

- 4 oz. canned salmon, drained, rinsed, and flaked
- ¼ c. lactose-free nonfat plain yogurt
- 1 tsp. grated orange zest
- 1 tsp. chopped fresh tarragon
- ½ tsp. sea salt
- 1 zucchini, cut into 12 rounds

Directions:

1. In a small bowl, combine the salmon, yogurt, orange zest, tarragon, and salt.

2. Spoon onto the zucchini rounds.

3. Serve.

Nutritional Info: Calories: 53, Protein: 7 g, Fat: 2 g, Carbs: 1 g

Olive Tapenade

Prep time: 15 minutes

Servings: 4

Ingredients:

- ½ c. pitted chopped black olives
- ½ anchovy fillet, chopped
- 1 tbsp. olive oil
- 2 tbsps. chopped fresh basil
- ½ tsp. lemon zest

Directions:

1. In a small bowl, mix all the ingredients until well combined.

2. Serve.

Nutritional Info: Calories: 51, Protein: 0 g, Fat: 5 g, Carbs: 1 g

Sweet Potato French Fries

Prep time: 10 minutes

Servings: 2

Ingredients:

- 1 sweet potato, peeled and cut into ¼-inch matchsticks
- 1 tsp. ground cumin
- ½ tsp. sea salt
- 1 tbsp. olive oil

Directions:

1. Preheat the oven to 450°F.

2. In a bowl, toss together the sweet potato sticks, cumin, salt, and olive oil.

3. Spread in a single layer on a rimmed baking sheet.

4. Bake, turning once with a spatula until the fries are browned and tender, about 20 minutes. Serve.

Nutritional info: Calories: 115, Protein: 1 g, Fat: 7 g, Carbs: 14 g

Artichoke Purée

Prep time: 10 minutes

Servings: 4

Ingredients:

- 14 oz. artichoke bottoms drained
- ½ c.low-fat rice milk
- 1 tbsp. unsalted grass-fed butter
- ½ tsp. sea salt

Directions:

1. In a small saucepan, combine all the ingredients. Cook over medium-high heat, occasionally stirring, until warm, about 5 minutes.

2. Transfer to a blender or food processor and blend until smooth.

3. Serve.

Nutritional Info: Calories: 134, Protein: 4 g, Fat: 10 g, Carbs: 12 g

Green Beans Amandine

Prep time: 10 minutes

Servings: 2

Ingredients:

- ¼ c. slivered almonds
- 24 green beans, trimmed and halved
- 1 tbsp. olive oil
- ½ tsp. grated lemon zest
- ½ tsp. sea salt

Directions:

1. Preheat the oven to 350°F.

2. Spread the almonds in a single layer on a rimmed baking sheet and bake until toasted, about 5 minutes.

3. Fill a large pot halfway with water and bring to a boil over high heat. Add the beans and cook, covered, until tender, about 4 minutes. Drain.

4. Toss the beans with the toasted almonds, olive oil, lemon zest, and sea salt. Serve.

Nutritional Info: Calories: 185, Protein: 5 g, Fat: 16 g, Carbs: 8 g

Roasted Asparagus with Goat Cheese

Prep time: 5 minutes

Servings: 2

Ingredients:

- 10 asparagus spears
- 1 tbsp. olive oil
- ½ tsp. sea salt
- 2 tbsps. crumbled goat cheese
- ½ tsp. grated lemon zest

Directions:

1. Preheat the oven to 425°F.

2. On a rimmed baking sheet, toss the asparagus with the olive oil and sea salt. Bake for 15 minutes or until tender.

3. Sprinkle with the goat cheese and lemon zest before serving.

Nutritional Info: Calories: 94, Protein: 3 g, Fat: 8 g, Carbs: 3 g

Creamed Spinach

Prep time: 5 minutes

Servings: 2

Ingredients:

- 1 bunch spinach, stemmed and chopped
- ½ tsp. sea salt
- ½ c. lactose-free nonfat milk
- 1 tsp. cornstarch

Directions:

1. In a large pot, add the spinach, and salt. Cook until the spinach is wilted, about 3 minutes.

2. In a small bowl, whisk together the milk and cornstarch. Add to the spinach. Cook, stirring, until the milk thickens, about 1 minute. Serve.

Nutritional Info: Calories: 135, Protein: 7 g, Fat: 8 g, Carbs: 13 g

Healthy Mashed Potatoes

Prep time: 10 minutes

Servings: 4

Ingredients:

- 2 russet potatoes, peeled and cubed
- ½ c. lactose-free nonfat milk
- 2 tbsps. unsalted grass-fed butter, at room temperature
- ½ tsp. sea salt

Directions:

1. Put the potatoes in a large pot and cover with plenty of water. Cover and cook over high heat until the potatoes are soft, about 15 minutes. Drain the potatoes and return them to the pot.

2. Add the milk, butter, and salt. Mash with a potato masher until smooth. Taste for seasoning and add more salt if necessary. Serve.

Nutritional Info: Calories: 136, Protein: 3 g, Fat: 6 g, Carbs: 21 g

Quinoa Pilaf

Prep time: 10 minutes

Servings: 4

Ingredients:

- 1 carrot, peeled and chopped
- ½ c. quinoa, rinsed
- 1 c. Simple Vegetable Broth
- ¼ c. pine nuts
- 2 tbsps. raisins
- 2 tbsps.freshly chopped parsley
- ½ tsp. sea salt

Directions:

1. Heat a medium pot over medium-high heat. Add the carrot with some broth and cook, occasionally stirring, until it starts to brown, about 5 minutes.

2. Add the quinoa and the remaining vegetable broth. Reduce to a simmer, cover, and cook until the quinoa is soft about 15 minutes.

3. Add the pine nuts, raisins, parsley, and salt just before serving.

Nutritional Info: Calories: 171, Protein: 4 g, Fat: 8 g, Carbs: 23 g

Roasted Honey-Ginger Carrots

Prep time: 5 minutes

Servings: 2

Ingredients:

- 4 large carrots, peeled and quartered
- 2 tbsps. honey
- 1 tbsp. olive oil
- 1 tsp. grated fresh ginger
- ½ tsp. salt

Directions:

1. Preheat the oven to 425°F.

2. Put the carrots in a single layer on a rimmed baking sheet.

3. In a small bowl, whisk together the honey, olive oil, ginger, and salt.

4. Drizzle over the carrots, turning to coat.

5. Bake until the carrots are tender, about 20 minutes. Serve.

Nutritional Info: Calories: 186, Protein: 1 g, Fat: 7 g, Carbs: 32 g

Chopped Kale Salad

Prep time: 15 minutes

Servings: 2

Ingredients:

- 2 c. stemmed and chopped kale
- 3 radishes, chopped
- 1 carrot, peeled and chopped
- ¼ c. lactose-free nonfat plain yogurt
- 1 tsp. Dijon mustard
- 1 tsp. chopped fresh thyme
- 1 tsp. chopped fresh dill
- ½ tsp. grated orange zest
- ½ tsp. sea salt

Directions:

1. In a large bowl, toss together the kale, radishes, and carrot.

2. In a small bowl, whisk together the yogurt, mustard, thyme, dill, orange zest, and sea salt.

3. Toss the dressing with the salad to serve.

Nutritional Info: Calories: 73, Protein: 4 g, Fat: <1 g, Carbs: 13 g

Quick Pasta Salad

Prep time: 15 minutes

Servings: 4

Ingredients:

- 2 c. cooked gluten-free elbow macaroni
- 1 c. baby spinach
- ¼ c. canned chickpeas
- ¼ c. sliced black olives
- ¼ c. chopped fresh basil
- 1 recipe creamy herbed dressing

Directions:

1. In a large bowl, toss together the macaroni, spinach, chickpeas, olives, and basil.

2. Toss with the dressing and serve.

Nutritional Info: Calories: 152, Protein: 7 g, Fat: 2 g, Carbs: 27 g

Coconut Rice Pudding

Prep time: 5 minutes

Servings: 4

Ingredients:

- Dried figs, ¼ c.
- Honey, 2 tbsps.
- Grated large pear, 1.
- Cooked brown rice, 2 c.
- Shredded coconut, ¼ c.
- Fat-free and sugar-free vanilla pudding mix, 1 oz.
- Ground ginger, ½ tsp.
- Low-fat milk, ¾ c.
- Low fat coconut milk, ½ c.

Directions:

1. Cook grated pear with milk, coconut milk, and honey in a pan on medium heat.

2. Boil the mixture then remove it from the heat.

3. Gradually stir in pudding mix, coconut, ginger, and rice.

4. Mix well and let this mixture sit for 10 minutes.

5. Stir in figs and mix gently.

6. Serve.

Nutritional Info:Calories: 190, Fat: 6 g, Carbs: 31 g, Protein: 3 g

Vanilla Parfait

Prep time: 10 minutes

Servings: 2

Ingredients:

- Sliced almonds, ¼ c.
- Greek fat-free yogurt, 1 c.
- Vanilla, 1 tsp.
- Chia seeds, ¼ c.
- Agave, 2 tbsps.
- Kosher salt, 1/8 tsp.
- Sliced Figs, 2 c.
- Unsweetened low-fat vanilla milk, 1 c.
- Agave, 4 tsp.

Directions:

1. Mix milk, yogurt, agave, vanilla, and salt in a medium bowl.

2. Whisk in chia seeds and let it rest for 25 minutes.

3. Cover the bowl and refrigerate it overnight.

4. Mix figs with agave and toasted almonds in a bowl.

5. Layer the serving glasses with yogurt pudding and figs alternatively.

6. Serve.

Nutritional Info: Calories: 199, Fat: 7 g, Carbs: 7.2 g, Protein: 4.7 g

Coconut Biscotti

Prep time: 10 minutes

Servings: 6

Ingredients:

- Baking soda, ¼ tsp.
- Egg whites, 2.
- Baking powder, ¾ tsp.
- Vanilla extract, 1 tsp.
- Flaked sweetened coconut, 1 c.
- Coconut Flour, 1 ½ c.
- Splenda, ¾ c.

Directions:

1. Set the oven to 300 degrees F to preheat.

2. Mix all the ingredients in an electric mixer to form a smooth dough.

3. Knead the dough then make 3-inch rolls out of this dough.

4. Place the rolls on the baking sheet lined with parchment paper.

5. Lightly press each roll and bake for 40 minutes at 300 degrees F.

6. Allow them to cool then diagonally slice the rolls.

7. Bake for another 20 minutes.

8. Serve.

Nutritional Info: Calories: 237, Fat: 19.8 g, Carbs: 55.1 g, Protein: 17.8 g

Almond Milk

Prep time: 10 minutes

Servings: 6

Ingredients:

- 2 c. almonds, peeled, soaked
- 6 c. water
- ½ vanilla bean, seeds removed

Directions:

1. Pour water into the blender.
2. Add soaked almonds and vanilla bean.
3. Blend it until smooth.
4. After this, strain the almond mixture with the cheesecloth and serve the almond milk.
5. Enjoy!

Nutritional Info: Calories: 183, Fat: 15.8 g, Carbs: 6.8 g, Protein: 6.7 g

Snack Avocados

Prep time: 7 minutes

Servings: 2

Ingredients:

- 1 avocado, pitted, halved
- 2 tsps. hemp seeds
- 1 tsp. olive oil

Directions:

1. Sprinkle the avocados with the hemp seeds.
2. After this, sprinkle the avocados with the olive oil.
3. Enjoy!

Nutritional Info: Calories: 229, Fat: 22, Carbs: 9.8, Protein: 2

Almond Toasts

Prep time: 5 minutes

Servings: 4

Ingredients:

- 4 slices gluten-free rye bread
- 1 tsp. olive oil
- 4 tsps. almond butter

Directions:

1. Sprinkle the bread slices with the olive oil and toast over a medium heat for 30 seconds from each side.

2. Spread the toasts with the almond butter.

3. Enjoy!

Nutritional Info: Calories: 130, Fat: 10.4 g, Carbs: 7.3 g, Protein: 4.1 g

Nut Bag

Prep time: 6 minutes

Servings: 4

Ingredients:

- 1 oz. almonds
- 1 oz. Brazil nuts
- 1 tsp. olive oil
- 1 tsp. salt

Directions:

1. Crush the almonds, and Brazil nuts gently and sprinkle them with salt.

2. Preheat the oven to 365 F.

3. Place the nut mixture on the tray and sprinkle with the olive oil. Stir well.

4. For 8 minutes, cook the nuts in the preheated oven, and stir from time to time.

5. Then chill the nuts till they are room temperature and transfer to a paper bag.

6. Enjoy!

Nutritional Info: Calories: 142, Fat: 13.8 g, Carbs: 3.6 g, Protein: 3.6 g

VEGETARIAN AND VEGAN

Potato Medley Soup

Prep time: 10 minutes

Servings: 4

Ingredients:

- Stock, 3 c.
- Oil, 1 tbsp.
- Potato, 2/3 lb.
- Fresh herbs.
- Chopped raw vegetables, ½ lb.

Directions:

1. Sauté vegetables with potatoes in a greased cooking pot until soft.

2. Stir in stock and bring it to a simmer.

3. Cook for 15 minutes then blend until smooth.

4. Serve warm with fresh herbs on top.

Nutritional Info: Calories: 304, Fat: 30.6 g, Carbs: 21.4 g, Protein: 4.6 g

Spaghetti with Watercress and Pea Pesto

Prep time: 10 minutes

Servings: 4

Ingredients:

- Watercress, ¼ c.
- Vegetarian fat-free hard cheese, ¼ c.
- Wholemeal spaghetti, 3 ¼ c.
- Egg whites, 4.
- Olive oil, 2 tbsps.
- Frozen peas, 2 c.

Directions:

1. Heat water to a simmer in a cooking pan and then add peas.
2. Cook for 3 minutes, drain, and then set it aside.
3. Blend peas with watercress and cheese until it forms into a thick paste.
4. Add olive oil and blend again until smooth.
5. Meanwhile, boil spaghetti as per the given instructions then drain and keep it aside.
6. Add water to a suitable cooking pot and bring it to simmer.
7. Create a whirlpool in the water and egg whites into it. Cook for 3 minutes.
8. Mix pesto with spaghetti and serve with poached egg whites and watercress on top.

Nutritional Info: Calories: 341, Fat: 4 g, Carbs: 16.4 g, Protein: 0.3 g

Vegetable Soup

Prep time: 10 minutes; Servings: 4

Ingredients:

- Golden caster sugar, ¼ tsp.
- Olive oil, 3 tbsps.
- Rosemary sprig, 2.
- Chopped carrot, 1.
- Chopped celery stick, 1.
- Vegetable stock, 3 c.
- Bay leaves, 2.
- Cauliflower florets, ½ lb.
- Shredded white cabbage, ¼ lb.
- Sliced gluten-free sourdough bread, ½ lb.
- Caraway seeds, 1 tbsp.
- Chopped potato, 1.
- Worcestershire sauce, 1 tsp.

Directions:

1. Set the oven to 320 degrees F to preheat.

2. Spread the bread baking tray along with caraway seeds, sea salt, and one tablespoon oil.

3. Bake for 10 minutes until golden.

4. In a large pot, add in carrot, potato, and the remaining olive oil.

5. Cook for 5 minutes until soft.

6. Stir in celery, seasoning, sugar, stock, bay leaves, thyme, and rosemary.

7. Boil the mixture then reduce the heat to a simmer.

8. Cook for 10 minutes then add cabbage and cauliflower.

9. Cook for another 15 minutes until al dente.

10. Stir in Worcestershire sauce.

11. Discard bay leaves, thyme, and rosemary and serve warm.

Nutritional Info: Calories: 418, Fat: 3.8 g, Carbs: 13.3 g, Protein: 5.4 g

Simple Vegetable Broth

Prep time: 10 minutes

Servings: 8

Ingredients:

- 2 carrots, peeled and chopped
- 1 leek, green part only, chopped and washed
- 1 celery stalk, chopped
- 1 fennel bulb, chopped
- 9 c. water

Directions:

1. In a large pot, combine all the ingredients.
2. Bring to a simmer over medium-high heat then lower the heat to low and simmer for 2 hours.
3. Strain the vegetables from the broth and store the broth until you're ready to use it.

Nutritional Info: Calories: 1, Protein: 0g, Fat: 0 g, Carbs: 3 g

Miso Soup with Tofu and Greens

Prep time: 10 minutes

Servings: 4

Ingredients:

- 1 leek, green part only, chopped and washed
- 3 oz. extra-firm tofu, cubed
- 7 c. Simple Vegetable Broth, divided
- 3 c. baby spinach
- 2 tbsps. miso paste

Directions:

1. In a large nonstick pot, add the leek and tofu and cook, stirring occasionally, until the leek is soft, about 5 minutes.
2. Add 6 cups of broth. Bring to a simmer and lower the heat to medium.
3. Add the spinach. Cook for 3 minutes.
4. In a small bowl, whisk together the remaining 1 cup of broth and the miso paste. Stir into the hot soup. Cook for 30 seconds more, stirring. Serve.

Nutritional Info: Calories: 117, Protein: 8 g, Fat: 6 g, Carbs: 12 g

Italian Vegetable Soup

Prep time: 10 minutes

Servings: 4

Ingredients:

- 1 leek, green part only, chopped and washed
- 1 carrot, peeled and chopped
- 1 chopped zucchini
- 1 c. green beans, trimmed and chopped
- 1 c. canned kidney beans
- 1 tbsp. dried Italian seasoning
- ½ tsp. sea salt
- 7 c. Simple Vegetable Broth
- 2 tbsps. chopped fresh basil

Directions:

1. In a large nonstick pot, add the leek, carrot, and zucchini and cook, occasionally stirring, until the leek is soft, about 5 minutes.
2. Add the green beans, kidney beans, Italian seasoning, salt, and vegetable broth. Bring to a simmer then lower the heat to medium. Simmer, stir occasionally, until the green beans are tender, 5 to 7 minutes.
3. Stir in the basil before serving.

Nutritional Info: Calories: 120, Protein: 5 g, Fat: 4 g, Carbs: 18 g

Creamy Pumpkin Soup

Prep time: 10 minutes

Servings: 4

Ingredients:

- 1 leek, green part only, finely chopped and washed
- 1 c. canned pure pumpkin
- 3 c. Simple Vegetable Broth
- 1 tsp. dried sage
- ½ tsp. sea salt
- ½ c. light coconut milk, nonfat
- 1 tsp. cornstarch

Directions:

1. In a large saucepan, add the leek and cook, stirring, until soft, about 5 minutes.
2. Add the pumpkin, vegetable broth, sage, and salt. Bring to a simmer and cook for 5 minutes.
3. In a small bowl, whisk together the coconut milk and cornstarch.
4. Remove the pan from the heat and carefully pour the soup into a blender or food processor, along with the coconut milk and cornstarch. Allow the steam to escape through the hole in the blender lid or the food processor feed tube as you blend to avoid a buildup of pressure. Blend until smooth.
5. Return the soup to the pot and warm over medium heat for 2 minutes or until thick. Serve.

Nutritional Info: Calories: 92, Protein: 2 g, Fat: 5 g, Carbs: 10 g

Cream of Broccoli Soup

Prep time: 10 minutes

Servings: 4

Ingredients:

- 1 green leek, finely chopped and washed
- 3 c. broccoli florets
- 6 c. Simple Vegetable Broth
- ½ tsp. sea salt
- 1 c. lactose-free nonfat milk
- 1 tbsp. cornstarch
- ½ c. baby kale
- ¼ c. microgreens

Directions:

1. In a large pot, add the leek and broccoli and cook, stirring, until the leek is soft, about 5 minutes.
2. Add the vegetable broth and salt. Bring to a simmer. Lower the heat to medium and simmer, stir occasionally, until the broccoli is soft, about 5 minutes.
3. In a small bowl, whisk together the milk and cornstarch. Stir into the soup. Cook for a few minutes more, stirring, until the soup thickens slightly.
4. Garnish with the kale and microgreens (if using) and serve.

Nutritional Info: Calories: 127, Protein: 6 g, Fat: 4 g, Carbs: 19 g

Sweet Potato and Corn Stew

Prep time: 10 minutes

Servings: 2

Ingredients:

- 1 leek, finely chopped and washed
- 2 c. spinach
- 1 medium sweet potato, peeled and cubed
- ½ c. canned or frozen corn
- 3 c. Simple Vegetable Broth
- 2 tsps. cornstarch
- 1 tsp. dried cumin
- ½ tsp. sea salt
- 1 c. lactose-free nonfat plain yogurt
- ¼ c.freshly chopped cilantro

Directions:

1. In a large saucepan, add the leek and cook, stir occasionally, until soft, about 5 minutes.
2. Add the spinach, sweet potato, and corn.
3. In a bowl, whisk together the vegetable broth, cornstarch, cumin, and salt. Add to the pan and bring to a simmer.
4. Lower the heat to medium. Cook, stir occasionally, until the sweet potato is soft, about 10 minutes.
5. Stir in the yogurt and cilantro before serving.

Nutritional Info: Calories: 248, Protein: 8 g, Fat: 8 g, Carbs: 39 g

Broccoli and Cheese Baked Potato

Prep time: 10 minutes

Servings: 2

Ingredients:

- 2 russet potatoes
- 1 c. broccoli florets
- ½ tsp. sea salt
- ½ c. grated Cheddar cheese

Directions:

1. Preheat the oven to 350°F. Pierce the potatoes several times with a fork.
2. Bake the potatoes on a rimmed baking sheet for 1 hour. Add the broccoli to the pan in a single layer. Continue to roast for 30 minutes or until the potatoes are soft and the broccoli is tender.
3. Split the potatoes. Season with the salt and top with the broccoli and Cheddar. (Melt the cheese in the microwave for about 45 seconds, if desired.) Serve.

Nutritional Info: Calories: 247, Protein: 11 g, Fat: 10 g, Carbs: 30 g

Lentil Tacos

Prep time: 10 minutes

Servings: 4

Ingredients:

- 4 small corn tortillas
- 1 leek, green part only, chopped and washed
- 2 c. canned lentils
- ¼ c. Simple Vegetable Broth
- 1 tsp. ground cumin
- ½ tsp. ground coriander
- ½ tsp. sea salt
- ¼ chopped avocado
- ¼ c. chopped fresh cilantro

Directions:

1. Preheat the oven to 350°F. Wrap the tortillas in aluminum foil and put them in the oven to warm for 15 minutes.

2. Meanwhile, in a large saucepan, add the leek and cook until soft, about 5 minutes.

3. Add the lentils, vegetable broth, cumin, coriander, and salt. Bring to a simmer and then lower the heat to medium. Simmer, stir occasionally, for 5 minutes.

4. To serve, spoon the lentils onto the tortillas, and top with the avocado and cilantro.

Nutritional Info: Calories: 256, Protein: 9 g, Fat: 8 g, Carbs: 37 g

Zucchini and Carrot Frittata

Prep time: 10 minutes

Servings: 4

Ingredients:

- 1 carrot, peeled and chopped
- 1 zucchini, grated
- 4 large eggs
- 1 tbsp. chopped fresh thyme
- ¼ tsp. sea salt

Directions:

1. Preheat the broiler on high.

2. In a large nonstick skillet, add the carrot and cook, stir occasionally, until it begins to soften, about 3 minutes.

3. Add the zucchini and cook for 2 minutes.

4. In a medium bowl, whisk the eggs with the thyme and salt.

5. Spread out the vegetables evenly in the bottom of the skillet.

6. Carefully pour the eggs over the top. Lower the heat to medium.

7. Cook until the eggs begin to set around the edges, about 2 minutes. Using a spatula, carefully pull the set eggs away from the sides of the skillet. Tilt the skillet to distribute the uncooked egg into the space you've made. Cook until the eggs set around the edges again, 2 to 3 minutes more.

8. Transfer the skillet to the broiler. Broil until set on top, 2 to 3 minutes.

9. Cut into wedges to serve.

Nutritional Info: Calories: 116, Protein: 7 g, Fat: 9 g, Carbs: 4 g

Zucchini Ribbons with Parmesan Cream Sauce

Prep time: 10 minutes

Servings: 2

Ingredients:

- 3 small zucchinis, cut into ribbons with a vegetable peeler
- ½ tsp. sea salt
- ½ c. lactose-free nonfat milk (rice milk)
- ¼ c. grated Parmesan cheese

Directions:

1. In a large, nonstick skillet, add the zucchini and salt and cook, stir occasionally, until tender, about 4 minutes.

2. While the zucchini cooks, heat the milk in a small saucepan over medium heat. When it simmers, whisk in the Parmesan.

3. Cook the milk mixture, stirring, until smooth. Toss with the cooked zucchini and serve.

Nutritional Info: Calories: 177, Protein: 11 g, Fat: 11 g, Carbs: 12 g

Asian Veggie and Tofu

Prep time: 10 minutes

Servings: 2

Ingredients:

- ¼ c. Simple Vegetable Broth
- 1 tsp. miso paste
- ½ tsp. grated fresh ginger
- ½ tsp. grated orange zest
- ½ tsp. sea salt
- 6 oz. extra-firm tofu, cubed
- 1 leek, green part only, chopped and washed
- 2 carrots, peeled and chopped
- 2 c. chopped bok choy

Directions:

1. In a small bowl, whisk together the broth, miso, ginger, orange zest, and salt. Set aside.

2. Heat a large nonstick skillet over medium-high heat.

3. Add the tofu, leek, carrots, and bok choy. Cook, stir occasionally until the veggies begin to brown, 5 to 7 minutes.

4. Add the reserved sauce and bring to a simmer. Cook, stirring, until the sauce thickens, 3 to 4 minutes more.

Nutritional Info: Calories: 206, Protein: 11 g, Fat: 12 g

Vegetable and Tofu Rice

Prep time: 10 minutes

Servings: 4

Ingredients:

- 1 leek, green part only, finely chopped and washed
- 1 carrot, peeled and chopped
- ½ c. broccoli florets
- 3 oz. extra-firm tofu, chopped
- 1 tbsp. grated fresh ginger
- 3 c. cooked brown rice
- ¼ c. Simple Vegetable Broth
- 1 tsp. miso paste

Directions:

1. Heat a nonstick skillet over medium-high heat. Add the leek, carrot, broccoli, tofu, and ginger and cook, stirring, until the veggies are soft, about 5 minutes.

2. Add the rice.

3. In a small bowl, whisk together the broth and miso. Add to the rice.

4. Cook, stir until warmed through, 3 to 4 minutes more, then serve.

Nutritional Info: Calories: 189, Protein: 5 g, Fat: 6 g, Carbs: 30 g

SEAFOOD and POULTRY

Baked Herb Tilapia

Prep time: 5 minutes

Servings: 6

Ingredients:

- Dried oregano
- Tilapia fillets, 2.
- Sea salt.
- Olive oil spray
- Dried thyme
- Dried basil

Directions:

1. Set the oven to 350 degrees F.

2. Layer a baking sheet with foil and olive oil.

3. Arrange the fish in the baking sheet and top it with herbs, salt, and olive oil.

4. Bake for 15 minutes.

5. Serve.

Nutritional Info: Calories: 372, Fat: 1.1 g, Carbs: 4.9 g, Protein: 33.5 g

Coconut Panko Shrimp

Prep time: 10 minutes

Servings: 4

Ingredients:

- Deveined large shrimp, 2 lbs.
- Olive oil, 2 tbsps.
- Coconut flakes, 1 4 oz.
- Panko flakes, ½ c.
- Egg whites, 4.

Directions:

1. Mix panko with coconut flakes in a shallow bowl.

2. Beat egg whites in another bowl.

3. Dip the shrimps in the egg whites then coat with crumb mixture.

4. Arrange the shrimps in a greased baking sheet.

5. Bake for about 10 to 15 minutes until al dente.

6. Serve warm.

Nutritional Info: Calories: 557, Fat: 29 g, Carbs: 25 g, Protein: 47 g

Crab Cakes with Healthy Tartar Sauce

Prep time: 15 minutes

Servings: 2

Ingredients:

- 1 c. cooked baby shrimp
- ¼ c. lactose-free nonfat plain yogurt
- 1 tbsp.freshly chopped dill
- 1 tsp. grated lemon zest
- ½ tsp. sea salt
- 2 c. lump crabmeat, picked over
- 1 tbsp. olive oil
- ¼ c. Healthy Tartar Sauce

Direction:

1. In a blender or food processor, combine the shrimp, yogurt, dill, lemon zest, and salt. Blend until smooth.

2. Spoon into a medium bowl. Carefully fold in the crabmeat until well combined. Form into four patties.

3. Heat a large nonstick skillet over medium-high heat.

4. Add the patties. Cook until browned, 4 to 5 minutes per side.

5. Serve topped with the Healthy Tartar Sauce.

Nutritional Info: Calories: 231, Protein: 31 g, Fat: 9 g, Carbs: 5 g

Miso-Glazed Scallops

Prep time: 5 minutes

Servings: 2

Ingredients:

- ¼ c. pure maple syrup
- 1 tsp. miso paste
- ½ tsp. sea salt
- 8 sea scallops, tendons removed
- 1 tbsp. unsalted grass-fed butter

Directions:

1. In a small bowl, whisk together the maple syrup, miso, and salt.
2. Brush the scallops with the mixture.
3. In a large nonstick skillet, melt the butter over medium-high heat.
4. Add the scallops and cook until just opaque, about 3 minutes per side. Serve.

Nutritional Info: Calories: 214, Protein: 11 g, Fat: 7 g, Carbs: 30 g

Breaded Crispy Shrimp

Prep time: 5 minutes

Servings: 2

Ingredients:

- 1 c. gluten-free breadcrumbs
- 1 tsp. sea salt
- 1 tsp. dried thyme
- ½ tsp. ground mustard
- 2 large eggs
- 2 c. medium raw shrimp, peeled and deveined, tails removed

Directions:

1. Preheat the oven to 400°F.

2. In a small bowl, combine the breadcrumbs, salt, thyme, and mustard, mixing well.

3. Beat the eggs in a separate bowl.

4. Dip each shrimp first into the beaten eggs and then into the breadcrumbs, tapping off any excess coating. Place the shrimp in a single layer on a rimmed baking sheet.

5. Bake, turning once until the shrimp are golden brown, 10 to 12 minutes. Serve.

Nutritional Info: Calories: 307, Protein: 42 g, Fat: 8 g, Carbs: 12 g

Steamer Clams with Fennel

Prep time: 10 minutes

Servings: 2

Ingredients:

- 1 tbsp. unsalted grass-fed butter
- 1 fennel bulb, cored and chopped, fronds reserved
- 1 leek, green part only, chopped and washed
- 2 lbs. steamer clams
- 2 c. Simple Vegetable Broth
- Grated zest of 1 lemon
- ½ tsp. sea salt

Directions:

1. In a large pot, melt the butter over medium-high heat.

2. Add the fennel bulb and leek and cook, stir occasionally, until soft, about 5 minutes.

3. Add the steamer clams, broth, lemon zest, and salt. Cover and cook until the clams open, about 5 minutes. (Discard any that did not open.)

4. Chop the fennel fronds and stir them into the broth. Serve.

Nutritional Info: Calories: 164, Protein: 11 g, Fat: 7 g, Carbs: 17 g

Halibut and Veggie Packets

Prep time: 10 minutes

Servings: 2

Ingredients:

- 1 zucchini, sliced
- 6 oz. halibut halved
- 1 tsp. grated lemon zest
- 1 tsp. dried dill
- ½ tsp. sea salt
- 2 tbsps. unsalted grass-fed butter, cut into two parts

Directions:

1. Preheat the oven to 350°F.

2. Place two 12-inch squares of parchment paper on a rimmed baking sheet.

3. Divide the zucchini slices between the squares and top each with a piece of halibut. Sprinkle each with half of the lemon zest, dill, and salt. Top each with a pat of butter.

4. Fold the squares into packets and seal the edges with narrow folds. Place the baking sheet in the oven and bake until the halibut is flaky about 20 minutes. Serve.

Nutritional Info: Calories: 228, Protein: 24 g, Fat: 14 g, Carbs: 4 g

Tilapia with Cantaloupe Salsa

Prep time: 10 minutes

Servings: 2

Ingredients:

- 2 (3 oz.) tilapia fillets
- 1 tbsp. olive oil
- ½ tsp. dried cumin
- ½ tsp. sea salt
- ½ c. cantaloupe salsa

Direction:

1. Preheat the oven to 425°F.

2. Place the fish fillets on a rimmed baking sheet. Brush with the olive oil and sprinkle with the cumin and salt.

3. Bake until the fish flakes, 10 to 15 minutes.

4. Top each fillet with half of the salsa. Serve.

Nutritional Info: Calories: 152, Protein: 17 g, Fat: 8 g, Carbs: 4 g

Easy Tuna Melt

Prep time: 10 minutes

Servings: 2

Ingredients:

- 6 oz. water-packed tuna, drained
- 3 tbsps. lactose-free nonfat plain yogurt
- ½ tsp. sea salt
- 2 slices gluten-free sandwich bread, toasted
- ½ c. grated Cheddar cheese

Directions:

1. Preheat the broiler on high.

2. In a small bowl, combine the tuna, yogurt, and salt.

3. Place the toasted bread on a rimmed baking sheet and spread each with half of the tuna mixture.

4. Top with the Cheddar.

5. Broil until the cheese melts, 3 to 4 minutes, then serve.

Nutritional Info: Calories: 345, Protein: 32 g, Fat: 14 g, Carbs: 22 g

Maple-Glazed Salmon

Prep time: 10 minutes

Servings: 2

Ingredients:

- ¼ c. Simple Vegetable Broth
- ¼ c. pure maple syrup
- 1 tsp. miso paste
- 1 tsp. grated orange zest
- ½ tsp. sea salt
- 2 (3 oz.) salmon fillets

Directions:

1. Preheat the oven to 400°F.

2. In a medium bowl, whisk together the broth, maple syrup, miso, orange zest, and salt. Marinate the salmon in it for 5 minutes, turning the fish once.

3. Place the salmon on a rimmed baking sheet. Bake until the salmon is flaky, about 15 minutes. Serve.

Nutritional Info: Calories: 259, Protein: 17 g, Fat: 9 g, Carbs: 27 g

Salmon and Lentils

Prep time: 10 minutes

Servings: 2

Ingredients:

- 2 (3 oz.) salmon fillets
- ½ tsp. ground cumin
- ½ tsp. sea salt, divided
- 1 carrot, peeled and chopped
- 1 parsnip, peeled and chopped
- 1 c. canned lentils drained and rinsed
- 1 tbsp. chopped fresh dill
- 1 tbsp. chopped fresh curly-leaf parsley, for garnish (optional)

Directions:

1. Preheat the oven to 400°F.

2. Season the salmon with the cumin and ¼ teaspoon of sea salt.

3. Place the salmon on a rimmed baking sheet. Bake until the salmon is flaky, about 15 minutes.

4. Meanwhile, heat a small skillet over medium-high heat.

5. Add the carrot and parsnip and cook, stir occasionally, until brown, about 5 minutes.

6. Add the lentils and the remaining ¼ teaspoon of sea salt. Cook until heated through, about 4 minutes more.

7. Stir in the dill.

8. Serve the salmon spooned over the lentils.

9. Garnish with parsley (if using) and serve.

Nutritional Info: Calories: 358, Protein: 24 g, Fat: 17 g, Carbs: 30 g

Fish Tacos with Guacamole

Prep time: 10 minutes

Servings: 4

Ingredients:

- 4 corn tortillas
- 8 oz. cod, skinned and cut into ½-inch pieces
- 1 tsp. grated lime zest
- 1 tsp. ground cumin
- ½ tsp. ground coriander
- ½ tsp. sea salt
- 1 c. grated Cheddar cheese
- ½ c. chopped fresh cilantro
- ½ c. guacamole

Directions:

1. Preheat the oven to 350°F. Wrap the tortillas in aluminum foil and put them in the oven to warm for 15 minutes.

2. Meanwhile, heat a large nonstick skillet over medium-high heat.

3. Add the cod, lime zest, cumin, coriander, and salt. Cook, stirring, until the cod is opaque and firm, about 5 minutes.

4. To assemble the tacos, divide the cod among the warmed corn tortillas. Top each with some Cheddar, cilantro, and guacamole. Serve.

Nutritional Info: Calories: 312, Protein: 23 g, Fat: 19 g, Carbs: 14 g

Fisherman's Stew

Prep time: 10 minutes

Servings: 2

Ingredients:

- 1 leek, green part only, chopped and washed
- 1 fennel bulb, cored and chopped, fronds reserved
- 6 oz. salmon, skinned and cut into ½-inch pieces
- ½ tsp. cornstarch
- 3 c. Simple Vegetable Broth
- 6 baby red potatoes, quartered
- 2 carrots, peeled and chopped
- ½ tsp. sea salt

Directions:

1. Heat a large pot over medium-high heat. Add the leek and fennel. Cook, stirring occasionally, until the vegetables start to brown, about 5 minutes.

2. Add the salmon and cook, stirring, for 3 minutes more.

3. In a small bowl, whisk the cornstarch into the broth, then add it to the pot, along with the potatoes, carrots, and salt.

4. Cook, stir occasionally until the potatoes are soft, about 10 minutes.

Chop the fennel fronds and stir them into the stew. Serve.

Nutritional Info: Calories: 420, Protein: 22 g, Fat: 17 g, Carbs: 49 g

Chicken Noodle Soup

Prep time: 10 minutes

Servings: 4

Ingredients:

- 1 tbsp. olive oil
- 1 leek, green part only, chopped and washed
- 1 carrot, peeled and chopped
- 1 chopped celery stalk
- 8 c. Poultry Broth
- 1 tsp. dried thyme
- 1 tsp. sea salt
- 1 oz. gluten-free spaghetti
- 8 oz. rotisserie chicken meat, skinless

Directions:

1. Heat a large pot over a medium-high heat. Add the leek, carrot, and celery. Cook, stir occasionally, until the vegetables start to brown, about 5 minutes.

2. Add the broth, thyme, and salt. Bring to a boil and add the spaghetti. Cook, stir occasionally until the spaghetti is soft, about 9 minutes.

3. Stir in the chicken and cook for 5 more minutes before serving.

Nutritional Info: Calories: 226, Protein: 22 g, Fat: 6 g, Carbs: 21 g

Baked Chicken Tenders

Prep time: 10 minutes

Servings: 2

Ingredients:

- 1 c. gluten-free breadcrumbs
- 1 tbsp. dried oregano
- 2 tsps. dried thyme
- ¾ tsp. sea salt
- ½ tsp. ground mustard
- 2 large eggs
- 6 oz. boneless, skinless chicken breast, cut into eight strips

Directions:

1. Preheat the oven to 425°F. Coat a rimmed baking sheet with nonstick cooking spray.

2. In a bowl, mix the breadcrumbs, oregano, thyme, salt, and mustard.

3. In a separate bowl, beat the eggs.

4. Dip the chicken strips into the eggs and then into the breadcrumb mixture, tapping off any excess coating.

5. Place the chicken tenders in a single layer on the prepared baking sheet. Bake until the chicken is golden brown, 15 to 20 minutes, then serve.

Nutritional Info: Calories: 233, Protein: 26 g, Fat: 7 g, Carbs: 16 g

Oven-Baked Chicken

Prep time: 10 minutes

Servings: 4

Ingredients:

- 1 c. gluten-free breadcrumbs
- 1 tbsp. dried thyme
- ¾ tsp. sea salt
- 3 large eggs
- 4 whole chicken legs without skin

Directions:

1. Preheat the oven to 350°F. Line a rimmed baking sheet with parchment paper or grease a baking sheet.

2. In a bowl, mix the breadcrumbs, thyme, and salt.

3. In a separate bowl, beat the eggs.

4. Dip the chicken legs into the eggs and then into the breadcrumb mixture, tapping off any excess coating.

5. Place in a single layer on the prepared baking sheet. Bake, turning once, until the chicken is golden brown, about 1 hour. Serve.

Nutritional Info: Calories: 293, Protein: 26 g, Fat: 18 g, Carbs: 7 g

One-Pot Chicken Stew

Prep time: 10 minutes

Servings: 4

Ingredients:

- 6 oz. boneless, skinless chicken breast, cut into ½-inch pieces
- 1 leek, green part only, chopped and washed
- 1 fennel bulb, chopped
- 1 c. chopped green beans
- 1 russet potato, cubed
- 5 c. Poultry Broth
- 1 tbsp. cornstarch
- 1 tsp. dried thyme
- ½ tsp. sea salt

Direction:

1. Heat a large pot over medium-high heat. Add the chicken, leek, and fennel and cook, stir occasionally until the chicken is cooked, about 5 minutes.

2. Add the green beans and potato.

3. In a small bowl, whisk together the broth and cornstarch. Add to the pot along with the thyme and salt. Cook, stirring occasionally, until the potatoes are soft, about 10 minutes more, then serve.

Nutritional Info: Calories: 179, Protein: 11 g, Fat: 5 g, Carbs: 19 g

Easy Turkey Burgers

Prep time: 10 minutes

Servings: 2

Ingredients:

- 6 oz. ground turkey breast
- ½ tsp. fish sauce
- 2 tsps. sugar
- ½ tsp. sea salt
- 2 gluten-free hamburger buns, toasted
- 4 tbsps. Healthy Burger Sauce

Directions:

1. In a medium bowl, combine the turkey breast, fish sauce, sugar, and salt. Mix well. Form into two patties.

2. Heat a large nonstick skillet over medium-high heat.

3. Add the turkey burgers and cook until browned on both sides, 6 to 7 minutes total.

4. Spread each bun with 2 tablespoons of Healthy Burger Sauce, and top with the turkey burgers. Serve.

Nutritional Info: Calories: 355, Protein: 25 g, Fat: 13 g, Carbs: 38 g

Turkey Meatballs

Prep time: 10 minutes

Servings: 2

Ingredients:

- ½ c. gluten-free breadcrumbs
- ½ c. lactose-free nonfat milk
- 6 oz. ground turkey breast
- ¼ c. chopped fresh cilantro
- 1 tbsp. grated fresh ginger
- 1 tsp. ground mustard
- ½ tsp. sea salt

Directions:

1. Preheat the oven to 375°F. Line a rimmed baking sheet with parchment paper or grease a baking sheet.

2. In a small bowl, combine the breadcrumbs and milk, and let sit for 5 minutes.

3. In a medium bowl, combine the turkey breast, cilantro, ginger, mustard, salt, and breadcrumb mixture. Combine well without overworking it (using your hands helps here).

4. Roll the mixture into 12 meatballs and place them on the prepared baking sheet.

5. Bake until the meatballs are cooked through, 15 to 20 minutes. Serve.

Nutritional Info: Calories: 158, Protein: 24 g, Fat: 2 g, Carbs: 12 g

Turkey Meatloaf Muffins

Prep time: 10 minutes

Servings: 4

Ingredients:

- 12 oz. ground turkey
- ¾ c. gluten-free breadcrumbs
- 1 large egg, beaten
- 1 tsp. Dijon mustard
- 1 tbsp. dried thyme
- ¾ tsp. sea salt

Directions:

1. Preheat the oven to 350°F. Coat a muffin tin with nonstick cooking spray.

2. In a medium bowl, combine all the ingredients.

3. Divide the mixture among four of the muffin cups. Bake until the internal temperature of the muffins is 165°F, about 20 minutes. Serve.

Nutritional Info: Calories: 136, Protein: 22 g, Fat: 3 g, Carbs: 6 g

Turkey and Spinach Rollatini

Prep time: 10 minutes

Servings: 4

Ingredients:

- 12 oz. boneless, skinless turkey breast, pounded ¼ inch thick
- ½ tsp. sea salt
- 1 c. frozen spinach, thawed
- 1 tsp. grated lemon zest
- ¼ c. crumbled feta cheese

Directions:

1. Preheat the oven to 325°F. Line a rimmed baking sheet with parchment paper or grease a baking sheet.

2. Place the turkey on the baking sheet, and sprinkle with the salt.

3. Spread the spinach over the turkey and sprinkle with the lemon zest and feta. Roll up the turkey around the filling and secure with either butcher's twine or presoaked toothpicks.

4. Bake until the internal temperature of the rollatini is 165°F, about 25 minutes. Cut crosswise into four sections to serve.

Nutritional Info: Calories: 214, Protein: 36 g, Fat: 5 g, Carbs: 4 g

Kale and Herb-Stuffed Turkey Cutlets

Servings: 4

Prep time: 15 minutes

Ingredients:

- ½ bunch kale, trimmed and chopped
- 1 tsp. dried thyme
- 1 tsp. sea salt, divided
- 4 (3 oz.) pieces turkey breast, pounded ⅜ inch thick
- 1 c. warmed mushroom gravy

Directions:

1. Heat nonstick skillet over medium-high heat. Add the kale, thyme, and ½ teaspoon of salt. Cook for about 5 minutes, stir occasionally until the kale is soft. Remove the kale from the pan and set it aside. Return the pan to the heat.

2. Season the turkey with the remaining ½ teaspoon of salt. Add it to the pan and cook for about 3 minutes per side until it is cooked through.

3. Top each piece of turkey with ¼ of the kale. Roll the turkey around the kale. Top each with a ¼ cup of gravy to serve.

Nutritional Info: Calories: 203, Fat: 9 g, Carbs: 12 g, Protein: 18 g

White Bean, Chicken, and Rosemary Casserole

Servings: 4

Prep time: 10 minutes

Ingredients:

- 8 oz. boneless and skinless chicken breast, cooked
- 2 c. canned white beans, drained
- 2 c. mushroom gravy
- 2 tsps. dried rosemary
- ½ tsp. sea salt

Directions:

1. Preheat the oven to 350°F.

2. In a large bowl, mix the chicken, beans, gravy, rosemary, and salt. Spoon the mixture evenly into four (6- to 8-ounce) ramekins.

3. Bake for 20 minutes. Serve.

Nutritional Info: Calories: 565, Fat: 16 g, Carbs: 37 g, Protein: 66 g

Shrimp and Grits

Servings: 4

Prep time: 10 minutes

Ingredients:

- 12 oz. medium shrimp, peeled and deveined
- 1 tsp. sea salt, divided
- 4 c. Poultry Broth
- 1 c. quick-cooking grits
- ¼ c. grated fat-free Cheddar cheese

Directions:

1. Heat the grill or a grill pan to medium-high heat.

2. Sprinkle the shrimp with ½ teaspoon of salt.

3. Grill the shrimp for about 4 minutes.

4. Meanwhile, in a medium saucepan over high heat, bring the broth and remaining ½ teaspoon of salt to a boil.

5. Stir in the grits. Return to a boil, stirring constantly. Reduce the heat to medium-low and simmer for 4 minutes, stirring frequently.

6. Stir in the cheese. Cook for about 2 minutes, stir constantly until the cheese melts.

7. Serve the grits topped with the shrimp.

Nutritional Info: Calories: 238, Fat: 9 g, Carbs: 14 g, Protein: 25 g

Broiled Shrimp

Servings: 2

Prep Time: 10 mins

Ingredients:

- 1 tsp. extra virgin olive oil
- ¾ lb. large shrimps shelled and deveined
- ½ tsp. dried rosemary, crushed
- Salt

Directions:

1. Preheat the broiler and place the rack 4 inches from the heat. Line a baking tray with foil.

2. Place the shrimp on the prepared baking tray in a single layer. Drizzle with the oil. Sprinkle the rosemary and salt over the shrimp.

3. Broil for about 3 to 4 minutes. Remove from the heat and serve warm.

Nutritional Info: Calories 101, Fat: 1.2 g, Carbs: 1.3 g, Protein: 19 g

Herb and Sour Cream Baked Halibut

Servings: 4

Prep time: 10 minutes

Ingredients:

- 4 (3 oz.) skinless halibut fillets
- ½ tsp. sea salt
- 1 c. fat-free sour cream
- 1 tbsp. chopped fresh dill
- 1 tbsp. chopped fresh parsley
- 1 tsp. dried thyme

Directions:

1. Preheat the oven to 350°F.

2. Line a rimmed baking sheet with parchment paper. Place the halibut fillets on the prepared sheet and sprinkle with the salt.

3. In a small bowl, mix the sour cream, dill, parsley, and thyme. Spread the mixture on the halibut.

4. Bake for about 20 minutes until the halibut flakes easily with a fork. Serve.

Nutritional Info: Calories: 152, Fat: <1 g, Carbs: 11 g, Protein: 22 g

BEEF and LAMB

Roast Rib of Beef

Prep time: 10 minutes

Servings: 6

Ingredients:

- Fresh sage leaves
- Olive oil, 1 tbsp.
- Peeled and halved carrots, 6.
- Small leeks, 5.
- Peeled and halved parsnips, 6.
- Extra-lean beef rib, 3lbs.
- Knorr beef stock cubes, 2.
- Peeled and halved shallots, 4.
- Sliced celery sticks.

Directions:

1. Set the oven to 400 degrees F.
2. Mix 1 Knorr beef cube with 1 tablespoon oil and rub this paste onto the beef.
3. Sear the beef in a greased pan until brown then transfer it to a roasting pan.
4. Sauté leeks in the same pan until golden and place them around the beef.
5. Now sauté carrots and parsnips in the pan and also transfer them to the roasting pan.
6. Top the beef with sage, celery, and shallots.
7. Bake for 45 minutes.
8. Serve.

Nutritional Info: Calories: 472, Fat: 11.1 g, Carbs: 19.9 g, Protein: 13.5 g

Vegetable Beef Soup

Prep time: 10 minutes

Servings: 4

Ingredients:

- 8 oz. extra-lean ground beef
- 1 leek, green part only, chopped and washed
- 1 carrot, peeled and chopped
- 1 fennel bulb, cored and chopped
- 1 c. halved green beans
- 7 c. Poultry Broth
- 1 tsp. dried thyme
- ½ tsp. sea salt

Directions:

1. In a large pot, add the ground beef, leek, carrot, and fennel and cook, stir occasionally, until the beef is browned and the vegetables are tender about 5 minutes.

2. Add the green beans, broth, thyme, and salt. Bring to a simmer then reduce the heat to medium and simmer for 5 minutes before serving.

Nutritional Info: Calories: 162, Protein: 13 g, Fat: 8 g, Carbs: 11 g

Pho with Zucchini Noodles

Prep time: 10 minutes

Servings: 4

Ingredients:

- 8 c. Poultry Broth
- 2 whole star anise
- 2 (1-inch) pieces peeled ginger
- ½ tsp. sea salt
- 3 zucchinis, cut into "spaghetti" noodles
- 8 oz. sirloin, chopped
- ¼ c. bean sprouts
- ¼ c. chopped fresh cilantro
- Grated zest of 1 lime

Direction:

1. In a large pot, combine the broth, star anise, ginger, and salt. Simmer over medium-high heat for 15 minutes. Remove and discard the anise and ginger.

2. Divide the zucchini noodles among four bowls and top with the sirloin strips.

3. Pour the hot broth over the noodles. Allow the broth to cook the noodles for 5 minutes.

4. Serve garnished with the bean sprouts, cilantro, and lime zest.

Nutritional Info: Calories: 161, Protein: 14 g, Fat: 8 g, Carbs: 6 g

Patty Melt Soup

Prep time: 10 minutes

Servings: 4

Ingredients:

- 1 tbsp. unsalted grass-fed butter
- 8 oz. extra-lean ground beef
- 1 leek, green part only, finely chopped and washed
- 8 c. Poultry Broth
- 1 tsp. ground mustard
- 1 tsp. ground caraway seeds
- ½ tsp. sea salt
- ½ c. grated Cheddar cheese

Directions:

1. In a large pot, melt the butter over medium-high heat. Add the ground beef and leek. Cook, crumbling the beef with a spoon, until it is browned for 5 to 7 minutes.

2. Add the broth, mustard, caraway seeds, and salt. Bring to a simmer. Cook for 5 minutes more.

3. Serve garnished with the Cheddar.

Nutritional Info: Calories: 197, Protein: 16 g, Fat: 11 g, Carbs: 4 g

Sirloin Steak Salad with Papaya Vinaigrette

Prep time: 10 minutes

Servings: 2

Ingredients:

- 1 tsp. ground cumin
- 1 tsp. dried oregano
- ½ tsp. sea salt
- 4 oz. sirloin steak
- 1 tbsp. olive oil
- 4 c. torn romaine lettuce
- 4 tbsps. papaya vinaigrette

Directions:

1. In a small bowl, combine the cumin, oregano, and salt. Season the steak on both sides with the spice mixture.

2. Heat a large nonstick skillet over medium-high heat. Add the sirloin. Cook for about 5 minutes per side for medium-rare.

3. Slice the steak and toss with the lettuce and papaya vinaigrette before serving.

Nutritional Info: Calories: 180, Protein: 13 g, Fat: 12 g, Carbs: 8 g

Inside-Out Cabbage Rolls

Prep time: 10 minutes

Servings: 2

Ingredients:

- 6 oz. extra-lean ground beef
- 1 leek, green part only, chopped and washed
- 2 c. chopped Napa cabbage
- 1 tsp. ground mustard
- 1 tsp. dried thyme
- ½ tsp. sea salt
- 1 c. cooked brown rice

Directions:

1. Heat a large nonstick skillet over a medium-high heat.

2. Add the ground beef, leek, cabbage, mustard, thyme, and salt. Cook, crumbling the ground beef with a spoon, until it is browned for about 5 minutes.

3. Add the rice. Cook to heat it through, about 4 minutes more, then serve.

Nutritional Info: Calories: 294, Protein: 22 g, Fat: 11 g, Carbs: 25 g

Hamburger Stroganoff with Zucchini Noodles

Prep time: 10 minutes

Servings: 2

Ingredients:

- 6 oz. extra-lean ground beef
- 1 c. sliced cremini mushrooms
- 1 leek, green part only, chopped and washed
- 1 tsp. dried thyme
- ½ tsp. sea salt
- 2 c. Poultry Broth
- 1 c. lactose-free nonfat milk
- 1 tbsp. cornstarch
- 2 small zucchinis, cut into ribbons

Directions:

1. Heat a large nonstick skillet over medium-high heat.

2. Add the ground beef, mushrooms, leek, thyme, and salt. Cook, crumbling the ground beef with a spoon, until it is browned, about 5 minutes.

3. In a small bowl, whisk together the broth, milk, and cornstarch. Add to the skillet along with the zucchini noodles and cook, stirring, until the sauce thickens slightly, about 2 minutes, before serving.

Nutritional Info: Calories: 291, Protein: 25 g, Fat: 10 g, Carbs: 22 g

Hamburger Stew

Prep time: 10 minutes

Servings: 4

Ingredients:

- 9 oz. extra-lean ground beef
- 1 leek, green part only, chopped and washed
- 2 carrots, peeled and chopped
- 1 c. corn kernels, fresh or frozen
- 1 russet potato, peeled and cubed
- 4 c. Poultry Broth
- 1 tbsp. cornstarch
- 1 tsp. dried thyme
- ½ tsp. sea salt

Directions:

1. Heat a large pot over medium-high.

2. Add the ground beef and leek. Cook, crumbling the ground beef with a spoon, until it is browned for about 5 minutes.

3. Add the carrots, corn, and potato.

4. Whisk together the broth, cornstarch, thyme, and salt. Add to the stew.

5. Cook, stir occasionally until the potatoes are tender, about 10 minutes, then serve.

Nutritional Info: Calories: 173, Protein: 14 g, Fat: 6 g, Carbs: 16 g

Beef Tacos

Prep time: 10 minutes

Servings: 4

Ingredients:

- 4 corn tortillas
- 1 tbsp. olive oil
- 9 oz. extra-lean ground beef
- 1 leek, green part only, chopped and washed
- 1 tsp. ground cumin
- 1 tsp. ground coriander
- ½ tsp. sea salt
- ½ avocado, chopped
- ½ c. grated Cheddar cheese
- ¼ c. Fat-free yogurt or sour cream

Directions:

1. Preheat the oven to 350°F. Wrap the tortillas in aluminum foil and heat in the oven for 15 minutes.

2. Meanwhile, heat a large nonstick skillet over a medium-high heat.

3. Add the ground beef, leek, cumin, coriander, and salt. Cook, crumbling the ground beef with a spoon, until it is browned for about 5 minutes.

4. To assemble the tacos, portion the beef on the tortillas. Top with the avocado, Cheddar, and sour cream. Enjoy!

Nutritional Info: Calories: 298, Protein: 19 g, Fat: 16 g, Carbs: 18 g

Flank Steak with Chimichurri

Prep time: 10 minutes

Servings: 4

Ingredients:

- 1 tsp. dried oregano
- 1 tsp. ground cumin
- ½ tsp. sea salt, divided
- 12 oz. flank steak
- 2tbsps. olive oil, divided
- ½ c. chopped fresh parsley
- ¼ c. chopped fresh cilantro
- Grated zest of ½ lime

Directions:

1. In a small bowl, stir together the oregano, cumin, and ¼ teaspoon of salt. Sprinkle evenly over the flank steak.

2. In a large nonstick skillet, add the flank steak and cook for 2 to 3 minutes per side.

3. Reduce the heat to low. Continue cooking until the steak it reaches 135°F for medium-rare, about 5 minutes more.

4. Meanwhile, in a blender or food processor, combine the remaining 2 tablespoons of oil, parsley, cilantro, lime zest, and remaining ¼ teaspoon of sea salt—pulse 20 times or until it is well combined.

5. Slice the flank steak thinly sliced against the grain. Serve with the chimichurri.

Nutritional Info: Calories: 276, Protein: 24 g, Fat: 20 g, Carbs: 1 g

Shepherd's Pie Muffins

Prep time: 10 minutes

Servings: 3

Ingredients:

- 6 oz.extra-lean ground lamb
- 1 leek, green part only, chopped and washed
- 1 carrot, peeled and chopped
- 1 c. green peas
- 1 tsp. dried thyme
- ½ tsp. sea salt
- 1 recipe of Healthy Mashed Potatoes
- ½ c. grated Cheddar cheese

Directions:

1. Preheat the broiler on high.

2. Heat a large nonstick skillet over medium-high heat.

3. Combine the ground lamb, leek, carrot, peas, thyme, and salt in the skillet. Cook, crumbling the lamb with a spoon until the vegetables are soft and the lamb is cooked for 5 to 7 minutes.

4. Divide the meat mixture evenly among four cups in a muffin tin. Top each muffin with mashed potatoes and sprinkle Cheddar over the top.

5. Broil until the cheese melts, about 3 minutes, then serve.

Nutritional Info: Calories: 361, Protein: 21 g, Fat: 24 g, Carbs: 42 g

Ground Lamb and Lentils

Prep time: 10 minutes

Servings: 4

Ingredients:

- 12 oz.extra-lean ground lamb
- 1 leek, green part only, chopped and washed
- 2 c. canned lentils
- 1 c. Poultry Broth
- 1 tbsp. ground cumin
- 1 tsp. ground coriander
- ½ tsp. sea salt
- 1 tsp. grated lime zest
- ¼ c. chopped fresh cilantro

Directions:

1. Heat a large pot over medium-high heat. Cook the ground lamb and leek, crumbling the meat with a spoon, until it is browned for about 5 minutes.

2. Add the lentils, broth, cumin, coriander, and salt. Cook, stir occasionally for 5 more minutes.

3. Serve garnished with the lime zest and cilantro.

Nutritional Info: Calories: 317, Protein: 21 g, Fat: 11 g, Carbs: 17 g

Herb-Crusted Lamb Chops

Prep time: 10 minutes

Servings: 2

Ingredients:

- ¾ c. gluten-free breadcrumbs
- 1 tbsp. unsalted grass-fed butter, at room temperature
- 1 tsp. Dijon mustard
- ¼ c. fresh rosemary leaves
- ¼ c. fresh oregano leaves
- ¼ c. fresh parsley
- ½ tsp. sea salt
- 4 extra-lean lamb loin chops

Directions:

1. Preheat the oven to 325°F.

2. In a blender or food processor, pulse the breadcrumbs, butter, mustard, rosemary, oregano, parsley, and salt 20 times, or until the herbs are chopped and well combined with the breadcrumbs.

3. Spread the mixture on the lamb chops, pressing, so it sticks to the surface of the meat.

4. In a large nonstick skillet, add the chops. Brown them for 3 minutes per side then transfer to a rimmed baking sheet.

5. Bake for 6 minutes or until the lamb reaches an internal temperature of 145°F. Serve.

Nutritional Info: Calories: 485, Protein: 21 g, Fat: 40 g, Carbs: 10 g

Roasted Lamb Chops with Chimichurri

Prep time: 10 minutes

Servings: 2

Ingredients:

- 4 extra-lean lamb loin chops
- ½ tsp. sea salt
- ½ c. oregano and parsley Chimichurri

Directions:

1. Preheat the oven to 325°F.

2. Season the lamb chops with the salt.

3. Heat a large nonstick skillet over medium-high heat.

4. Add the chops. Brown them for 3 minutes per side then transfer to a rimmed baking sheet.

5. Bake for 6 minutes or until the lamb reaches an internal temperature of 145°F.

6. Serve with the chimichurri spooned over the top.

Nutritional Info: Calories: 421; Protein: 46; Fat: 25 g; Carbs: 2 g

Open-Faced Stuffed Burgers

Prep time: 10 minutes
Servings: 4
Ingredients:

- ½ c. lactose-free nonfat milk
- ¼ c. gluten-free breadcrumbs
- 1 lb. extra-lean ground beef
- ½ tsp. sea salt
- 1 tsp. Dijon mustard
- ½ tsp. fish sauce
- ½ c. grated Cheddar cheese
- 4 tbsps.freshly chopped basil
- 4 slices gluten-free bread, toasted
- 4 tbsps. Healthy Burger Sauce

Directions:

1. In a small bowl, combine the milk and breadcrumbs. Allow it to rest for 10 minutes.

2. In a medium bowl, combine the ground beef, breadcrumb mixture, salt, mustard, and fish sauce until well mixed. Roll into eight balls and pat each out into a ¼-inch thick patty.

3. In a small bowl, mix the cheese and basil. Sprinkle the cheese mixture on each of four patties and top with another patty. Pinch the edges to seal.

4. Preheat a nonstick skillet on medium-high. Place the burger patties in the skillet and heat until cooked, about 5 minutes per side.

5. Serve on the toasted bread with 1 tablespoon of the Healthy Burger Sauce spooned over the top of each.

Nutritional Info: Calories: 366, Protein: 30 g, Fat: 17 g, Carbs: 24 g

SAUCES and CONDIMENTS RECIPES

Honey Mustard

Prep time: 5 minutes

Servings: 12

Ingredients:

- Honey, ¼ c.
- Stone-ground mustard, ½ c.

Directions:

1. Mix everything in a glass bowl.

2. Serve or store for later use.

Nutritional Info: Calories: 28, Fat: 1 g, Carbs: 6 g, Protein: 0 g

Arugula Pesto

Prep time: 5 minutes

Servings: 12

Ingredients:

- Stevia, 2 tsps.
- Water, 2 tbsps.
- Fresh arugula, 4 c.
- Olive oil, 2 tbsps.
- Pine nuts, 2 tbsps.
- Salt, ¼ tsp.

Directions:

1. Blend all the ingredients in a blender.

2. Serve.

Nutritional Info: Calories: 83, Fat: 8 g, Carbs: 1 g, Protein: 3 g

Beef Broth

Prep time: 10 minutes

Servings: 8 cups

Ingredients:

- 3 lbs. beef bones
- 3 carrots, chopped
- 1 fennel bulb, chopped
- 1 bay leaf
- 1 rosemary sprig
- 1 thyme sprig
- 9 c. water

Directions:

1. In a slow cooker, combine all the ingredients
2. Cover and simmer on low for 12 to 24 hours.
3. Strain out the solids. Refrigerate overnight.
4. In the morning, skim and discard the fat. Store in one-cup servings in the freezer for up to six months.

Nutritional Info: Calories: 20, Protein: 2 g, Fat: 0 g, Carbs: 2 g

Poultry Broth

Prep time: 10 minutes

Servings: 8

Ingredients:

- 1 carrot, peeled and chopped
- 1 leek, green part only, roughly chopped and washed
- 1 celery stalk, chopped
- 2 lbs. poultry bones
- 9 c. water

Directions:

1. In a large pot, combine all the ingredients.

2. Bring to a simmer over medium-high heat then lower the heat to low and simmer for 4 hours.

3. Strain the vegetables and bones from the broth and store the broth in the refrigerator overnight.

4. Skim the fat that has solidified on top of the broth and then discard it. Store the broth in 1-cup servings in the freezer until you're ready to use it.

Nutritional Info: Calories: 10, Protein: 0 g, Fat: 0 g, Carbs: 3 g

Papaya Vinaigrette

Prep time: 10 minutes

Servings: 4

Ingredients:

- ½ papaya, chopped
- 1 tbsp. olive oil
- ½ tsp. grated lemon zest
- 1 tbsp. chopped fresh thyme
- ½ tsp. sea salt
- ¼ c. water

Directions:

In a blender or food processor, combine the papaya, olive oil, lemon zest, thyme, and salt. Process until smooth, thinning with the water as needed.

Nutritional Info: Calories: 47, Protein: <1 g, Fat: 4 g, Carbs: 4 g

Healthy Tartar Sauce

Prep time: 5 minutes

Servings: 4

Ingredients:

- ½ c. lactose-free nonfat plain yogurt
- 2 tbsps. chopped fresh dill
- 1 tsp. grated lemon zest
- ½ tsp. sea salt

Directions:

In a small bowl, mix all the ingredients until well combined.

Nutritional Info: Calories: 20, Protein: 2 g, Fat:<1 g, Carbs: 3 g

Healthy Burger Sauce

Prep time: 5 minutes

Servings: 4

Ingredients:

- ½ c. lactose-free nonfat plain yogurt
- 1 tbsp. coconut aminos
- ½ tsp. fish sauce
- 2 tbsps. brown sugar
- 2 tbsps. chopped fresh thyme

Directions:

In a small bowl, mix all the ingredients until well combined.

Nutritional Info: Calories: 39, Protein: 2 g, Fat:<1 g, Carbs: 8 g

Lemon Yogurt Sauce

Prep time: 5 minutes

Servings: 4

Ingredients:

- ½ c. lactose-free nonfat plain yogurt
- 1 tsp. grated lemon zest
- ¼ tsp. sea salt

Directions:

In a small bowl, mix all the ingredients until well combined.

Nutritional Info: Calories: 17, Protein: 2 g, Fat:<1 g, Carbs: 3 g

Conclusion

Given that the causes of any specific person's heartburn and related GERD symptoms are likely to be fairly complex, as well as highly individual, it may well require a combination of these theories and recommended remedies to find relief.

One thing they all have in common is the belief that finding and treating the underlying cause, rather than the symptoms, provides the best solution for lasting relief. Get dirty in the kitchen by experimenting with the recipes in this book.

Dr. Jessika Schwab

IMPORTANT

for corrections, suggestions and comments:
drjessikaschwab.books@gmail.com

Acid Reflux Resources

Your doctor: Tell your doctor all your symptoms, the severity of the symptoms, and how long you've experienced them. Your doctor may or may not recommend over-the-counter medications such as antacids and may or may not prescribe medications. Either way, he's an ally in your battle against reflux. If your doctor doesn't take your symptoms seriously enough, find another physician.

American College of Gastroenterology: The American College of Gastroenterology (ACG) is an esteemed professional organization for gastroenterologists. The ACG website has lots of very helpful information for patients, including information on acid reflux, Barrett's esophagus, and more. You can even find a local physician affiliated with the ACG using the Physician Finder.

Academy of Nutrition and Dietetics: The Academy of Nutrition and Dietetics is for dietitians, but, like many of the other association websites in this list, it has helpful information for patients as well.

American Academy of Family Physicians: The website of the American Academy of Family Physicians (AAFP) is for physicians, but it also has information for patients.

International Foundation for Functional Gastrointestinal Disorders: The name says it all—this site covers disorders of the function, or mechanism, of the gastrointestinal (GI) tract. There's a bounty of information on acid reflux, GERD, and heartburn. These conditions are international, and so is the foundation. Reflux really gets around.

GIKids: This resource is great if you're trying to treat acid reflux in a child.

American Society for Gastrointestinal Endoscopy: The American Society for Gastrointestinal Endoscopy (ASGE) is another reputable, trusted education source for gastrointestinal specialists. The society also advances gastrointestinal medicine. Its website has lots of good information for patients.

American Gastroenterological Association: The American Gastroenterological Association (AGA) serves gastroenterology professionals and offers public information as well.

National Digestive Diseases Information Clearinghouse: The National Digestive Diseases Information Clearinghouse (NDDIC) is a government database of digestive-related topics, statistics and resources. The information is plentiful and trustworthy.

Food and Drug Administration: The Food and Drug Administration (FDA) has a lot on its plate. The administration's purpose is to keep the American public safe by monitoring the safety of—you guessed it—foods and drugs. The website covers a dizzying array of topics, including acid reflux, gastroesophageal reflux disease (GERD), and heartburn, and includes information on related drugs and drug trials.

https://my.clevelandclinic.org/health/articles/15530-lifestyle-guidelines-for-the-treatment-of-gerd

https://wakegastro.com/patient-info/gerd-diet/

https://www.aboutgerd.org/diet-lifestyle-changes/diet-changes-for-gerd.html

https://www.byrdie.com/natural-remedies-for-acid-reflux

https://www.chewfo.com/diets/dropping-acid-the-reflux-diet-cookbook-cure-2010-by-jamie-koufman-jordan-stern-and-marc-bauer-what-to-eat-and-foods-to-avoid-food-list/#induction

https://www.dailymail.co.uk/health/article-4174090/The-surprising-new-food-rules-banish-acid-reflux.html

https://www.drugs.com/drug-class/antacids.html

https://www.emedicinehealth.com/acid_reflux_disease_gerd/article_em.htm#what_is_gastroesophageal_reflux_disease_gerd

https://www.fishertitus.org/health/gerd-diet-plan

https://www.health.harvard.edu/diseases-and-conditions/herbal-remedies-for-heartburn

https://www.healthline.com/health/gerd

https://www.healthline.com/health/gerd/diet-nutrition

https://www.healthline.com/health/gerd/melatonin#1

https://www.healthline.com/nutrition/heartburn-acid-reflux-remedies

https://www.mayoclinic.org/diseases-conditions/gerd/symptoms-causes/syc-20361940

https://www.medicalnewstoday.com/articles/14085.php

https://www.medicalnewstoday.com/articles/146619.php

https://www.medicalnewstoday.com/articles/314531.php

https://www.medicalnewstoday.com/articles/314886.php

https://www.medicalnewstoday.com/articles/323170.php

https://www.nature.com/gimo/contents/pt1/full/gimo31.html

https://www.ncbi.nlm.nih.gov/pmc/articles/PMC3400817/

https://www.ncbi.nlm.nih.gov/pmc/articles/PMC4991651/

https://www.ncbi.nlm.nih.gov/pmc/articles/PMC5503285/

https://www.pccmarkets.com/sound-consumer/2008-08/sc0808-detox/

https://www.pritikin.com/acid-reflux-diet

https://www.tums.com/about-heartburn/quick-heartburn-relief/antacids/

https://www.verywellhealth.com/breakfast-menus-for-the-acid-reflux-diet-3575752

https://www.verywellhealth.com/remedies-for-heartburn-relief-89992

https://www.webmd.com/heartburn-gerd/guide/heartburn-gerd-basic-information-causes

https://www.webmd.com/heartburn-gerd/guide/lifestyle-changes-heartburn

https://www.webmd.com/heartburn-gerd/guide/understanding-gerd-treatment#1

https://www.webmd.com/heartburn-gerd/guide/what-is-acid-reflux-disease#1

https://www.youtube.com/watch?v=MCwiV1WbeiA

Made in the USA
Coppell, TX
21 November 2019

11696924R00115